Building Multicultural Churches

Valuing ethnic diversity

Tony Thompson

malcolm down
PUBLISHING

Copyright © Tony Thompson 2025
First published 2025 by Malcolm Down Publishing Ltd.
www.malcolmdown.co.uk

29 28 27 26 25   7 6 5 4 3 2 1

The right of Tony Thompson to be identified as the author
of this work has been asserted by him in accordance with
the Copyright, Designs and Patents Act 1988.

All rights reserved. No part of this publication may be reproduced,
stored in a retrieval system, or transmitted in any other form or by
any means, electronic, mechanical, photocopying, recording or
otherwise, without the prior permission of the publisher.

British Library Cataloguing in Publication Data
A catalogue record for this book is available from the British Library.

ISBN 978-1-917455-10-7

Unless otherwise indicated, Scripture quotations are taken from
the Holy Bible New International Version (Anglicised edition).
Copyright ©1979, 1984, 2011 by Biblica.
Used by permission of Hodder & Stoughton Publishers,
an Hachette UK company. All rights reserved.
'NIV' is a registered trademark of Biblica.
UK trademark number 1448790.

Scripture quotations marked 'ASV' are from the Holy Bible, American
Standard Version, which is in the public domain.

Scripture quotations marked 'Phillips' are taken from
The New Testament in Modern English by J.B. Phillips copyright ©
1960, 1972 J.B. Phillips. Administered by The Archbishops'
Council of the Church of England. Used by Permission.

Scripture quotations marked 'ESV' are taken from the Holy Bible,
English Standard Version (Anglicised). Published by HarperCollins
Publishers © 2001 Crossway Bibles, a publishing ministry of
Good News Publishers. Used by permission. All rights reserved.

Cover design by Esther Kotecha
Art direction by Sarah Grace

Printed in the UK

Endorsements

During the intense racial tensions that arose in our communities following the tragic murder of George Floyd by police in Minneapolis in May 2020, Tony Thompson stood out as a courageous individual. He bravely acknowledged the issue, took a stand, and called out racism. He was pivotal in initiating discussions, fostering reconciliation and advocating racial justice within the church community in Luton and wider afield.

Vincent Cox, Senior Pastor, New Testament Church of God (Luton)

The coalface is the best place to mine theology from. My friend Tony Thompson does so brilliantly in this timely book. His core question is how to build missional churches that authentically involve people and leaders from minority cultures in today's UK, but without patronising them. There are startlingly fresh insights from the Bible (including ways to read it well globally), and regular mention of contemporary issues such as immigration, asylum-seekers, Black Lives Matter, and 'woke' accusations ... Tony gives poignant examples from his church-planting ministry in Luton, and is refreshingly humble and disarmingly honest about his own wake-up calls from God ... Throughout, Tony makes great use of pictorial metaphors that have staying power ... Questions at the end of each chapter provoke further individual/group reflection, and there are plenty of action-points suggested ... On many occasions I had a personal 'Ouch!' moment, nudging me to ponder, 'Where do I too need to repent?', such repentance flowing from God's kindness to me ...

In my opinion, Tony is a prophetic trail-blazer, particularly as a white, male Brit and church leader. His book is one to trawl through and bring in a catch slowly, facing the pain in God's heart and human beings' hearts with a glistening sense of biblical hope for a better future. Can the mould be broken of heaps of homogeneous churches here in Britain? I am hopeful it can.

Andrew Whitman, lifelong pastor, watchful missiologist, and recent author of When Jesus Met Hippies: The Story and Legacy of the Jesus People Movement in the UK *(Malcolm Down Publishing)*

I am delighted to commend Tony Thompson for his exceptional work in the field of multicultural ministry and valuing of ethnic minority and diversity. It has been a joy to be working with Tony within Churches Together in Luton to promote unity within and across churches. Tony's insightful book, *Building Multicultural Churches,* provides a valuable resource for churches seeking to embrace diversity and foster inclusive communities.

Tony's understanding of the importance of valuing the perspectives of those from different ethnicities and traditions makes this impressive and valued work of his possible. He demonstrates a deep understanding of the challenges and opportunities inherent in multicultural contexts. His work is characterised by a commitment to social justice, equality, equity and reconciliation. He has a unique ability to connect with people from diverse backgrounds, creating safe spaces where individuals feel valued and empowered.

I commend Tony for his tireless efforts to promote common and intercultural understanding and cooperation among multicultural communities. His faith and contributions to the field of theology and ministry and as the current chair of the Churches Together in Luton have had a significant impact on countless individuals, congregations and communities in Luton town.

Rev. Patrick Gbanie Kandeh MA, BA (Hons), CTM, CTPS
Superintendent Methodist Minister, South Bedfordshire Circuit

Tony is someone who dedicates his whole self to bringing out the best in people across our diverse town. He brings people from all cultures, ages and religions together to work on shared aims and for the realisation that there is more that unites than divides us. Tony is a force for good.

Sarah Owen, MP for Luton North

Contents

Introduction	9
1. Understanding the Biblical View of Unity and Diversity	27
2. The Challenges the Early Church Faced: Antioch	45
3. The Impact of Prejudice	63
4. Principalities and Powers: Prejudice Viewed as Spiritual Warfare	79
5. The Role of Multicultural Church in Evangelism	97
6. The Importance of Humility	109
7. Understanding Culture	127
8. Understanding Things from a Minority Perspective	147
9. Justice	161
10. Reading the Bible with Blinkers Removed	173
11. Drawing Things to a Close	183

Introduction

The 1945 British Nationality Act formalised the reality that everyone part of the British Empire was in fact British, and resulted in a wave of immigration. The consequence of this is that the United Kingdom is increasingly diverse, which is impacting everyone. Some rejoice in the increase of diversity, others do not. Whatever our stance, diversity is here to stay and is growing. Official data shows that diversity in the UK grew by over two and a half times between the 2001 and 2021 census, from 2.02 to 5.14 RDI (the official measure of diversity).[1]

Initially the UK church was not universally welcoming to the early immigrants. This lack of welcome and the natural tendency for those newly arrived to worship with those from a similar background meant that churches remained almost exclusively monocultural.

However, churches in the UK are now becoming more diverse at a faster rate than the nation as a whole. This is due to many factors, including the fact that ethnic minorities

---

1. https://theconversation.com/census-data-shows-england-and-wales-are-more-ethnically-diverse-and-less-segregated-than-ever-before-197156 (accessed 9.10.24).

who had previously travelled long distances to attend a church with others from their own background are choosing to worship more locally. This can be because they now feel more integrated in general society, or even if they don't, their children do. Others are seeing weakness in monocultural churches, especially in leadership, which can be perceived as reflecting the weaknesses of that culture. Another factor is the relatively large number of Christians from minority ethnic groups; research in 2022 found 25 per cent of practising Christians came from minority groups compared to 12 per cent of the general population.[2]

Many churches now welcome this growth; however, beyond the initial warm welcome, they struggle to know how to embrace diversity, people who are different from me. It is hard work to think through the implications for worship, leadership and even how to build relationships with those who are different from us. But unless we grapple with these issues, we will not see the fullness of that which God desires for us. It is into this context I want to write. I hope you will find this book helpful as you seek to build churches that embrace all that God has for us, which I believe goes much further than just celebrating having many different nations as part of our worshipping communities. Much further than displaying national flags in the name of unity.

The convictions out of which I write

This book is designed to help you understand the importance of the calling to work towards a united church that celebrates

---

[2]. https://talkingjesus.org/research (accessed 9.10.24).

and honours diversity. A church that values unity while moving on from uniformity. It also seeks to give pointers of how this might be achieved, to raise questions, provoke thinking and to add to the current debate.

I believe that God's ideal is a church which demonstrates how life will be at the end of the age, where people from 'every nation, tribe, people and language' are worshipping together as equals (Revelation 7:9), welcoming all into this community of faith. For this to happen we must first recognise the prejudices we hold and address them. We might see ourselves as victims of prejudice, but we all pre-judge others, making us all both victims and perpetrators of prejudice. It is healthy to admit this and to explore this ourselves, with God and with others if we are to move on to God's ideal for his church.

I write as a white male Christian leader, who led a multicultural church in a multicultural town, Luton, which is thirty miles north of London. The current population of around 225,000 people is a third Muslims, a third white British and a third other nationalities.

I write out of a conviction that the dividing wall of hostility between different groups has been destroyed in Christ to create 'one new humanity' in him (Ephesians 2:14-15). His (God's) 'intent was that now, through the church, the manifold wisdom of God should be made known to the rulers and authorities in the heavenly realms, according to his eternal purpose that he accomplished in Christ Jesus our Lord' (Ephesians 3:10-11). I believe that wisdom of God is found in the coming together of people from different ethnic and social backgrounds bringing their distinct contribution to the family of God.

However, despite what God is doing in creating diverse churches, most churches in Luton are still monocultural, despite (or maybe because of) the great diversity that exists in Luton. As well as bringing the challenge of 'What should a church gathering people from different backgrounds look like?', I also want to challenge monocultural churches and to ask the question, 'Is that God's intention?' Whatever the monoculture is.

I am convinced that God's ideal is for each individual church to bring together people from different backgrounds and to celebrate those differences. While working and praying for this ideal, I am also convinced that in the meantime we need to work together as leaders and as churches from different backgrounds, to learn from each other and together to demonstrate the 'manifold wisdom of God'.

I am also convinced that we should be demonstrating and modelling God's intention to the world. With John Perkins, a veteran civil rights leader from the USA, I believe that 'there is no institution on earth more equipped and capable of bringing transformation to the cause of reconciliation than the church. But we have some hard work to do'.[3] I also agree with Tom Wright who says in his essay 'Undermining Racism' that we have failed in our vocation in bringing about this reconciliation:

> Paul in Colossians 3.11 insists that in the Jesus-following family there is neither Jew nor Greek, circumcised or not, Barbarian, Scythian, slave or free. That's what it

---

3. John M. Perkins, *One Blood: Parting Words to the Church on Race and Love* (Chicago, IL: Moody, 2018), Kindle edition, p. 63.

means, he says, to put on the New Humanity, which is being renewed in knowledge according to the image of the creator. This dream was regularly ignored in western churches in the modern period, but was then picked up in the secular Enlightenment. Today's secular vision of a multicultural global society is at its best a Christian ideal detached from its Christian roots. The Christian churches, by and large, left out a big element in the understanding and application of their own central faith. The secular world has picked it up. This is typical of various cultural moves that have been made in the last two or three hundred years. God, one might reflect, doesn't lack witnesses. If the church doesn't speak up, others may do it instead. Sometimes, as Jesus warned, the children of this age are wiser than the children of light.[4]

It annoys me when friends suggest that somehow, I and others are being caught up in the world's 'woke' agenda, using that as an argument to avoid addressing issues. Unfortunately, this happens far too often, in fact most times I speak on the subject! Instead, we should receive the challenge presented to us by the world as a rebuke that we have not been leading the way in bringing reconciliation and speaking truth. We should not just criticise and dismiss 'wokism', but we urgently need to present a Christian alternative.

I am also challenged by the insight from Malawian theologian based in the UK, Harvey Kwiyani, who compares his experience growing up in Africa with his experience in the UK:

---

4. https://ntwrightpage.com/2020/06/14/undermining-racism-complete-text/ (accessed 19.09.24). Permission received.

Worship in the congregations where my parents live happens in a mixture of languages. It is common for people to sing Lhomwe and Yao songs in worship, say their intercession in chiSena or chiTumbuka, and then listen to a sermon in chiChewa . . . Our segregated Christianity is an anomaly, and it is my sincere hope that we will not export it to the rest of the world like we have other aspects of our Christianity in the past.[5]

We have so much to learn from our brothers and sisters in Christ from different parts of the world, which we will see as the book unfolds.

I am also convinced that we need to give weight to the fact that when Paul talks about us being 'one in Christ' (Galatians 3:28-29, see also Colossians 3:11), he uses the examples of ethnic, social and gender divisions being broken down. My experience is that the three go together and that we need to fight for God's ideal at all three levels. I could add a fourth, that of disability. Too often we have failed in all these areas. Walls of hostility need to be broken down; reconciliation needs to be worked for in each. When we do so we bear witness to the Good News of Jesus to a needy world. While acknowledging the importance of valuing all kinds of diversity, I will primarily be focusing on ethnic diversity while recognising the principles apply more widely.

There are many more books written about multicultural church and the importance of racial reconciliation from an American context than from a UK perspective. While we

---

[5]. H.C. Kwiyani, *Multicultural Kingdom: Ethnic Diversity, Mission and the Church* (London: SCM, 2020), Kindle edition, p. 10. Permission received.

have much to learn from our US cousins, our context is very different. We cannot just take their experience and translate it into our context. Additionally, there are many more books written by authors from a minority perspective than from a majority context. These too are valuable, and I have learned so much from them. My experience is that too often the points raised by ethnic minorities are not fully listened to, they can be dismissed as people having a 'chip on their shoulder'. Therefore, I am convinced that as a white male working and living in the UK, I am not disqualified from contributing to the discussion but that I too have a unique and important contribution to make.

I recognise that I do not have all the answers but hope that what I write will make a helpful contribution.

My background and journey

This book is the result of a long personal journey of discovery. A dictionary definition of racism is that if you describe people, things or behaviour as racist, you mean that they are influenced by the belief that some people are inferior because they belong to a particular race. By that definition I grew up in a racist family and inherited racist views. Growing up in the 1960s such views didn't seem out of place. Everyone seemed to have them. Indeed, many of the TV programmes from the late sixties and early seventies would now greatly offend our values and worldview.

As I look back, I am truly ashamed of not just my views but both my actions and lack of actions that resulted from them. As a teenager I was bullied but I was also a bully myself, to the only boy from a Pakistani background in the school, until one day he asked me why I was doing it. I had no answer and stopped. I remembered seeing a young girl from a Caribbean background being assaulted, but rather than being revolted I was fascinated by it.

Now hearing stories of what life was and is like for people from minority ethnic backgrounds, I am revolted by my contribution to the damage and pain that racist attitudes and actions cause. I have sincerely repented of such attitudes and have asked for forgiveness where possible. Repentance is more than just saying or feeling sorry; it is about changing one's attitude and seeking to make amends. That is what I have been seeking to do in the last decade or so. This book is part of that repentance, sharing my journey and seeking to help others to go on a similar journey.

Not only do I have a history of racial prejudice, I am aware of taking for granted my privileges, that of being educated, being a male and being white. I did not question that privilege; I did not even recognise it and I certainly didn't seek to use it to the good of those who did not share my good fortune.

I grew up in a working-class family in Luton in the 1960s. My parents were not churchgoers, having both left the church as young teenagers, but they would have called themselves Christians. I was therefore christened in the local Anglican church, but only attended church a few times before I left Luton to go to university. I was the first member of my family to go on to further education. My childhood experience of church was not positive; it felt irrelevant to my life, something for weddings and funerals and maybe at Christmas. I had one school friend who was a Christian; he was a very kind boy, but I saw him as weak!

Introduction

At university I started arguing with Christians, arrogantly feeling that I could convince them of the error of their belief. To my surprise I concluded that they were right, and I was wrong. That Jesus really did rise again from the dead and if that happened, as he said it would, then I had to take everything else he said seriously. I remember grappling with the implications of this for a few days, then concluded that to not accept Christ was the same as rejecting him. I couldn't do that; my first ever real prayer was, therefore, 'Alright, God, I give in.'

Initially I thought this just meant that I was now on a different side of the argument, but I soon realised it meant far more than that. Not only was there a God who created me, he loved me and had revealed himself to me. To begin with this seemed too good to be true. However, I hadn't wanted it to be true but had been convinced that it was true. Therefore, my whole view of the world needed to change. No longer could I make a God in my own image but had to acknowledge the God who had revealed himself in Christ Jesus. I also had to reluctantly accept it meant going to church.

I struggled to fit in with church and Christians. A friend took me to various churches but there seemed to be more people in the choir than in the congregation. I couldn't work out when to stand up and when to sit down. I seemed out of step with everyone else in so many ways. I also struggled to fit into the organisation through which I had become a Christian. They disapproved of advice I had given to a friend who had also just started following Jesus. I knew I could no longer be part of that organisation, but this left me feeling isolated from my Christian friendship base.

These very early experiences as a Christian led me to feel I didn't fit in the church. There was an underlying feeling of being an outsider that continued for decades, and took many years to leave me completely. I wasn't always consciously aware of it. Over time I was very fortunate to find some great people and churches that were very kind to me and supported me in my walk with Christ. My relationship with God was strong and I persevered with church despite feeling an outsider at times.

I now realise that my experience is not uncommon; many people struggle to feel at home, to feel valued and accepted and understood in church. At one stage I concluded that church was for those brought up in church, people who understood the rules that I didn't. I was also convinced that many of those rules were man-made and were not consistent with what I was reading in the Bible. What I saw in Scripture I found attractive and, more importantly, true. It was how the truth of Scripture was worked out that gave me difficulty. I therefore sought to base my faith on Scripture and read as many commentaries on the Bible as I could get my hands on. I felt my ignorance but was hungry to grow and learn. Interestingly I never felt my racial prejudice being challenged in what I read.

The most important thing is that I persevered – too many people do not.

This experience was formative in my thinking, and I have since concluded that churches that embrace and value people from many different backgrounds and perspectives are in a much better position to understand Scripture and how it is to be applied than those that are monocultural.

Introduction

Many years after leaving university, I felt God speak to me about going into church leadership full-time. This initially resulted in me becoming part of the leadership team of the church where I worshipped, and then on the staff team as the church evangelist. I went to Bible college part-time.

The consensus from those around me at church was that I was ill-equipped to lead a church; it was mentioned on numerous occasions – I was too rough round the edges. I was much better suited to being a church evangelist. Therefore, the Bible college course was in evangelism and church planting, alongside a theology degree. However, God had other ideas. During one lecture at college, it was suggested that the model for church leadership hadn't changed since the Victorian age where 90 per cent of the population were linked with a church, and pastoral evangelism was the order of the day. Now with only 10 per cent of the population linked with a church, there was a need for us to experiment with a new model of church leadership, one that equipped the 10 per cent to reach the 90 per cent. I came out of that lecture no longer feeling disqualified from leading a church, but that people like me should be leading churches.

I might have been convinced, but others were not. Looking back, I realise all sorts of options were presented to me rather than to lead something, like a new church plant. When it became clear that I really needed to be given the opportunity to test my call, I was released to start a new church in St Neots, a small market town between Bedford and Cambridge. I was blessed to be supported by a fantastic team, especially those sent as co-leaders, Tony and Barbara Hassall.

The new church, Open Door Church, St Neots, flourished and grew. By the time that I left Open Door Church, a third of those who were part of the community were not from churchgoing backgrounds. The church was predominantly white British, but so was the town. However, it included people from different social classes being family together.

I realise that God had prepared and equipped me for this, to be a bridge between those brought up in church and those who had not been. To be a bridge between middle-class people and working-class people. Overcoming feelings of not fitting in was not just for my sake, but to enable me to help other outsiders fit in. It was a battle at times, but I knew God was with me.

In the early days we had to be very purposeful. In naming the church Open Door Church we wanted to make a prophetic statement. However, after the first year we had laid a good foundation, we were viable, but were only gathering Christians, some having moved into the area, others worshipping closer to home. I believe this to be valid – we were not 'sheep stealing', everyone else felt very happy with this, but somehow, I wasn't; I knew this was not all that God had called us to. I found out the hard way that you can be leading a church you wouldn't want to be a member of! We had to battle with God in prayer and then put things in place to enable us to reach out beyond ourselves, otherwise we would have been just like any other church. Having the right preparation and the right intention, I realised, was not enough. There needed to be prayer and accompanying action to see desires come to fulfilment. Breaking new ground is hard work.

These were lessons I took with me to Luton.

The call to Luton came out of the blue. There were many different elements of the call, including remembering an experience from the first few months after I became a Christian. In the weeks after my conversion, on a return visit from university, I spent a morning prayer walking around the area of Luton I had grown up in. I was crying out to God for both the local churches and my friends, as there was no connection between them. I had totally forgotten doing it, but in prayer God took me back to that experience and I felt him say that I was going to be used as part of the answer to my own prayer. This was one of many ways I felt God was speaking to me.

Naively, I assumed that what had been built in St Neots could be replicated in Luton. I had no real understanding of what church should look like in a multicultural, working-class town with a large Muslim population. I really didn't give it any thought or prayer. God had taught me through the time in St Neots how to reach out; I just assumed we could see the same fruit with the same strategy in Luton. We couldn't, and it took many years before we started to see fruit.

Once again, I was part of a strong committed team of fellow pioneers that joined together to serve God in Luton. Some came from St Neots, others purposely getting jobs in Luton after university and others already living in the town. As part of our planting team, we had two cousins, Linda and Sonya, from a Sri Lankan Asian background. They, with the rest of us, wanted to plant an outward-looking multicultural church. None of us had any idea how it would happen! We just assumed it would occur. I had forgotten the lesson of being purposeful that I had learned in St Neots. Looking back, both Linda and Sonya would say that they had learned to supress their Eastern background to be accepted in church cultures. They had learned to assimilate without being conscious of doing so. In a similar way, I realised that I had become middle class, no longer displaying characteristics of the working-class background I had grown up in. We were a monocultural middle-class planting team with little awareness of how to attract people from the other cultures that were prevalent in Luton.

I found myself leading a church that wasn't yet expressing God's heart for diversity, and it left me feeling uncomfortable. This time it took much longer for me to even understand why that was and what the church God wanted us to plant in Luton should look like, and then even longer to see it take shape.

The breakthrough started when we began to attract a handful of people from different ethnic backgrounds. Each felt called to be part of a majority white church and were willing to pay the cultural price in doing so. They started to invite others, so that eventually we looked less white. For them this was a sacrifice that I didn't fully understand. It is said that you need at least 20 per cent of people to be from different backgrounds from the majority culture for other minorities to feel comfortable to join you. That took us many years to achieve.

Things accelerated when we were able to purchase our own building on the outskirts of the town centre. It was close to the red-light district in Luton. Previously it had been a Polish social club and well known as a wedding and party venue. For a few years it had not been used and we were able to purchase it at a price we could just about afford, thanks to the sacrificial generosity of members, a large mortgage and a year of hard work from a team renovating it. When we bought the building, the bottom car park had a discarded mattress that was regularly used. During the year of renovation, it was not unusual to see couples walking down the side of the building to be surprised by people working and the mattress gone. There needed to be regular cleaning of used condoms, which is still the case.

Getting the building established emphasised the fact that we were there for the long haul. Its position meant that we started to attract many more people who were not middle class. We could finally begin the journey of establishing a church where there is 'neither Jew nor Gentile, neither slave nor free, nor is there male and female, for we are all one in Christ Jesus' (Galatians 3:28). We had people from different ethnic backgrounds and different social classes. This was a starting point, a foundation from which we could create a community where everyone was valued for who they are and what they bring. As a church we want to fully appreciate everyone for their unique contribution. To move beyond assimilation.

We are still on that journey, but I feel we are far enough along to be able to share some of the lessons we have learned on the way. To encourage others to be intentional about creating churches that truly reflect the age that is to come.

We all have a part to play in enabling this to happen, leaders and non-leaders, white, brown and black, middle class and working class. We can all make that purposeful decision that the church should be a model of unity, being one in Christ, while celebrating our diversity and seeking to learn from each other.

Recently we identified that we want to be a church that:

- Sees people of all cultures as a blessing, and that we are complete together and recognise we can all learn from one another.
- Submits joyfully to alternative cultural patterns and styles.
- Is enriched through friendship with those from many cultures.
- Celebrates language diversity and makes room for their use.
- Intentionally builds an environment where leadership decisions are influenced by the perspectives of different cultures.
- Speaks out against discrimination.

We are not there yet, but at least we know where we want to be. I want to encourage and excite you to want to be part of a church on a similar journey. I want to share lessons I have learned on the way, helping you avoid my mistakes. I am convinced that our nation needs to be re-evangelised. I am convinced that the church has a contribution to bring to a divided world. I am convinced that this will be done by churches that demonstrate life in 'the age to come' (Matthew 12:32) in the present, churches that demonstrate unity in diversity.

The purpose of this introduction is to introduce myself to you, to let you know that mine is a long and not straightforward journey. To share some initial thoughts: there are no quick fixes; the importance of welcoming new people into our churches and helping them feel part of the family; the need for churches to be clear and purposeful about what they feel God is calling them into – just having a vision doesn't mean it all happens; probably the most important lesson is that ultimately we are dependent on the grace of God – ultimately he is the one in control and we can trust him.

Questions to ponder

- In what ways would you see yourself as a victim and perpetrator of prejudice?
- How convinced are you that a priority for Christians is to remove the barriers that exist between different ethnic groups and different social classes?
- Can you think of a small step you can take to broaden your understanding of those from a different background to yourself?

1.

Understanding the Biblical View of Unity and Diversity

Despite having followed Christ for many decades, reading my Bible most days and even having a theology degree, it is only recently that I have gained more than a cursory understanding of how the Bible helps us to understand cultural and ethnic differences. These truths were hidden in plain sight as far as I was concerned. Maybe this is true for you too.

I can't give a full Bible study on the subject, but hopefully in this chapter I can give a flavour of what the Bible says about celebrating and valuing both unity and diversity, and why we should make it a priority as we build churches.

God as three in one

When looking at the Bible we need to start with God, who reveals himself to us as three in one, Trinity – see John 1:1-3. Our understanding of God as Trinity is the best place to start when valuing our unity in Christ as well as our distinctives.

The orthodox understanding of Trinity is that God is one and yet exists in three equal, eternal and distinct persons. 'God is not more three than one, nor more one than three. He is perfect unity in diversity and diversity in unity.'[6] If that is the nature of God, we should expect to see this reflected in his creation, especially in humankind, made 'in the image of God' (Genesis 1:27).

We should value each person regardless of race, ethnicity, class, gender or age in the same way as we value each member of the Trinity. If God displays his beauty in Trinity, we should expect that beauty to also be displayed in the expanse of humanity created in his image.

The ideal of creation made in the image of God was shattered by the Fall

God created a single race, the human race. We are introduced to Adam, but are nowhere told the colour of his skin. I guess it is very easy to just assume it would be white.

Our understanding of different races is a relatively recent introduction used to justify slavery. It was coined by 'white' people to identify 'higher' and 'lower' races. Interestingly, or maybe disturbingly, when Irish and Italians entered the US in large numbers in the nineteenth century they were not seen as white! Eventually they were admitted into the dominant group. I therefore seek to avoid using the term 'race' other than the human race, as it is unnecessary and has such a chequered history with regards to slavery and colonisation. Why use such a loaded term if you don't have to?

---

6. See for example https://gospelinlife.com/article/the-bible-and-race/ (accessed 9.10.24).

What is useful is to look at how the Bible helps us understand the proliferation of language and ethnicities. I have found Andy McCullough in his book *Global Humility: Attitudes for Mission* very helpful in this.

In Genesis 10 we have a list of the descendants of Noah, following the flood. After each genealogy the author tells us that there were distinct clans and nations, each with their own language (10:5,20,31). However, when we come to 11:1 we read: 'Now the whole world had one language and a common speech.' It is an obvious question to ask: what happened to create a common language out of the many?

In chapter 10:8-12 we are introduced to Nimrod the son of Cush who was 'a mighty warrior' and the founder of an extensive kingdom and a great city as its capital. Andy and others suggest that Nimrod has done what so many tyrants after him through history chose to do: he has implemented one state language, quashing tribal expression and sentiment, outlawing the indigenous. It was this empire that said, 'Come, let us build ourselves a city, with a tower that reaches to the heavens, so that we may make a name for ourselves; otherwise we will be scattered over the face of the whole earth' (Genesis 11:4). The Lord's response is to scatter the people and re-establish the original separate languages.

The significant point that is not always understood or appreciated, is that multiplicity of languages is a blessing not a curse. It was part of God's intention prior to the tower of Babel, prior to the first empire. Nimrod and those like him see the value of a common language, and often a common culture. Colonisation is not a modern invention. Currently, in many parts of the world it is English and American language and culture that has dominated. That is not God's intention.

As we will see throughout Scripture, not only does he value diversity, but he is the author of it. A similar point can be made from the creation story, where he made humankind, man and woman to complement each other and to become one flesh. Unity and diversity equally valued.

Unity out of diversity, unity without losing diversity is God's intention. Humankind's natural inclination is to squash diversity and make everything the same. That is especially true of the powerful, even within the church! Hence from very early on in church history this, in my opinion, obvious understanding of Genesis 11 has not been widely taught.

This understanding of Genesis 10 and 11 impacts how we understand the events recorded in Acts 2 when the Spirit fell on the day of Pentecost. People heard the gospel in their own language – God again actively giving value to the plurality of language.

The outworking of this in our churches

Humankind's tendency is still, like Nimrod, to seek to gather to one centre, to build, to homogenise, and the Spirit's tendency is still to scatter, to diversify. This is seen throughout church history, humankind seeking to create a unified church without valuing diversity. The Spirit then blowing that false unity apart, such as with Martin Luther, William Tyndale and other reformers who championed translating the Scriptures into local languages, enabling God's intention of diversity over uniformity. The Spirit doesn't just value and initiate diversity, the Spirit is also the Spirit of unity. It is therefore also worth noting that the times there was the greatest unity in the American church were in times of revival. Black and white gathered to hear Wesley and Whitefield preach during the Methodist revival in the eighteenth century. They then worshipped together in the same church. It was only after the revival that separate churches were formed for black and white worshippers. We now have a proliferation of black and white Methodist denominations. The same happened during the Pentecostal revival centred on the black church in Azuza Street, Los Angeles. Black and white met God together, with diverse leadership; it was only after the revival fires died that the church became segregated again.[7]

This has massive implications for the type of church we want to build in the multicultural towns and cities that dominate today. Do we want to build united churches with a common language and culture? Or do we want to build churches that celebrate and value diversity, that recognise the value of different cultures?

I think we are also meant to see the contrast between Nimrod and his followers who sought to 'make a name' for themselves (Genesis 11:4) while God promised Abram that he would make a name for him (12:2). As Andy McCullough says:

> Humans keep wanting to get their identity and honour from being part of something big, something visible, some tangible measures of success, yet God keeps calling us to leave those things behind and trust him for honour and a name.[8]

---

7. See William K. Kay, *Pentecostalism: A Very Short Introduction (Very Short Introductions)* (Oxford: OUP, 2011), Kindle edition, chapter 2.
8. Andy McCullough, *Global Humility: Attitudes for Mission* (Milton Keynes: Malcolm Down Publishing, 2017), Kindle edition, p. 91.

It is so much easier to build and be part of churches where we have a common culture and language, whether that is white English church or a Nigerian Yorùbá church. They are more likely to grow bigger; however, the question we need to keep asking is whether that is God's intention? Is that us making a name for ourselves rather than for God? I have become convinced that the 'narrow way'[9] of unity while valuing diversity is the better way, the way that glorifies God. I am also convinced that such churches are the ones that will ultimately make a difference in our nation.

Other Old Testament examples of the importance of diversity and how easily we miss it

God promised Abraham that all the people of the earth would be blessed through him (Genesis 12:3). Every time Abraham got things wrong, the promise was repeated in different forms – see for example 17:5: 'I have made you a father of many nations', and 22:18: 'All nations on earth will be blessed.' As Daniel Hayes says, 'Part of God's redemptive plan as revealed in Genesis is to save and bless individuals from all peoples of the earth and to reunite them as the people of God. Racialization or racial division in the Church thwarts the plan of God and is in direct disobedience to this central biblical theme.'[10]

We see the outworking of this promise in the Exodus, where Moses led the descendants of Abraham out of slavery in Egypt. I think it is highly significant that in Exodus 12:38 we

---

9. See Matthew 7:13-14.
10. J. Daniel Hays, *From Every People and Nation* (Downers Grove IL: IVP, 2003), p. 63.

read that 'many other people', a mixed crowd, presumably Egyptians and slaves of other ethnicities, went up with them. This would probably include black Africans from Cush. As the people of God went towards the promised land, they were already a diverse people. Israel from its very early days was not an ethnically pure community.[11] This diversity continued throughout the history of the people of God as described in the Old Testament.

We keep finding people from lots of different ethnicities playing key roles. Moses marries a Midianite woman, Zipporah (Exodus 2) and then a black African from Cush (Numbers 12:1). Moses' interracial marriage is not approved of by Aaron and Miriam, but the Lord makes it very clear that he approves. There are regular instructions against intermarriage, but these are to prevent the children serving foreign gods, not against interracial marriage as such (see for example Deuteronomy 7:1-4); the issue is marrying outside of the faith, not about ethnicity.

A Cushite (a black African) is given the responsibility by Joab of telling David that his son Absalom was dead (2 Samuel 18). Another Cushite, Ebed-Melek, is an official in the king of Judah's palace who comes to Jeremiah's aid in Jeremiah 38.

Prominent roles are played by foreign women, for example, Rahab and Ruth, so prominent that they are included in the genealogy of Jesus in Matthew 1:5. Surely the reason Matthew includes them is to demonstrate the importance of the nations through Jesus' mixed heritage. Matthew is widely acknowledged as writing for a Jewish audience.

---

11. Hays, *From Every People and Nation*, p. 68.

Diversity within the New Testament – in Luke

Time doesn't permit a full analysis of the theme of diversity in the New Testament as it is everywhere, but it is worth looking at a few examples to see how pervasive the topic is.

A quick trip through Luke's Gospel shows chapter after chapter how ethnic and social expectations and assumptions are turned upside down. Luke, in contrast to Matthew, was thought to be writing to a Gentile audience.

In chapter 1 we are meant to contrast the priest Zechariah with the teenage Mary. Mary unexpectedly is seen as being godlier than her older, male, priestly relative. In the next chapter the birth of Christ is proclaimed to shepherds who were at the very lowest point of the social order (2:8-20). Then in chapter 3 the direct descendants of Abraham are threatened with being replaced by stones (3:7-9). The great prophets Elisha and Elijah are introduced, healing not Israelites but a despised widow and a foreign soldier (4:25-27). A despised tax collector, Levi, is invited to become an insider in 5:27-32. Outsiders, the poor and oppressed are blessed in 6:20-26, while the rich and those who are spoken well of are cursed. Jesus eats at the home of Simon the Pharisee, where he welcomes and praises a woman who has lived a sinful life while appearing to demonstrate that the Pharisee is really the outsider (7:36-50). The common crowd are called his 'mother and brothers' in 8:19-21; Jesus declares children are to be welcomed in 9:46-50. In chapter 10 the hero of the parable is a despised Samaritan (10:25-37). The men of Nineveh are said to rise in judgement and condemnation against 'this generation' in 11:32. Chapter 12 describes the rejection of a rich man, contrasted with the abundant treasures belonging to those who sell their possessions and give to the needy (12:13-21). Chapter 13 describes how various people who would expect to enter the kingdom of God will be excluded while others from around the world will be included (13:29). The parable of the great banquet describes how those initially invited are replaced by the poor, crippled, blind and lame (14:13). The younger sinful son is included while the older son excludes himself in the parable in Luke 15:11-31. Lazarus the beggar rather than the rich man enters heaven in 16:19-27; only the Samaritan of the ten lepers who were healed returns to Jesus and praises God in 17:15-19. The hated tax collector goes home justified rather than the Pharisee in the parable in 18:9-14. Zacchaeus the chief tax collector receives Jesus into his home and receives salvation in 19:1-10. The vineyard, the symbol of the people of God, is given over to other tenants (Gentiles) in the parable in 20:9-19. Then in 21:1-4 the poor widow is commended in contrast to the rich people.

In every chapter in Luke, until the last week of Jesus' life, we see outsiders included into the people of God. For those who have eyes to see, it seems clear that we are meant to see the inclusive nature of the kingdom; it is for everyone, whatever ethnicity, social class, or gender. Luke is making the same point as Paul when he says that we are all one in Christ, whether Jew, Gentile, slave, free, male or female (Galatians 3:28). Yet it is so easy to miss it.

> All through Luke, outsiders are in and insiders are out. Tax collectors, prostitutes, Gentiles, Samaritans, children,

'sinners', younger sons: 'in'. Teachers of the law, scribes, Pharisees, lawyers, the dutifully religious, the socially respected, older sons: 'out' ... In today's terms, Jesus came to seek and to save sex workers, pimps, dishonest corporate leaders, welfare dependents, convicted felons, crooked journalists, drug addicts, disenfranchised ethnic minorities, social rejects, the homeless, the smelly, the disgusting.[12]

I would want to add the important role that women play in Luke, which for some reason Ortlund (above) doesn't mention.

Diversity in John

We find very similar truths in John's Gospel, which we will look at very briefly.

Very early in the Gospel John says, 'But Jesus would not entrust himself to them, for he knew all men. He did not need man's testimony about man, for he knew what was in a man' (John 2:24-25, NIV 1984).

Following this we find encounters between Jesus and various representatives of humankind, which develop the idea that men cannot be fully trusted – Nicodemus, a Samaritan woman and an official's son are the main characters used by John to do this. I think we are meant to compare the three. Nicodemus is the only one named; he is the one with all the advantages, he is the insider. Yet he just doesn't get it. In contrast the unnamed outsiders

---

12. Dane C. Ortlund, *Surprised by Jesus: Subversive Grace in the Four Gospels* (Leyland: Evangelical Press, 2021), Kindle edition, p. 94.

do get it; they are the examples of what it means to follow Jesus. The person you expect to get it, the important, named Pharisee, doesn't understand, yet in contrast the despised outsiders do.

Andy McCullough develops this by saying:

> Like the other Gospel writers, John makes Jesus' mission to the marginalised a major theme of his writing. Christ, declaring himself to be the new Temple, focuses on taking the temple to those who cannot come, on being the temple to those who are socially, ethnically or religiously barred from access. The Samaritan woman, the official's son, the crippled man, the woman caught in adultery, the blind man, all are marginalised, disregarded, dehumanised by the Jerusalem elite, and all are brought dignity by Jesus.[13]

John and Luke through their Gospels are pointing their readers to see God at work in people who are not like us. To see God at work in people who you wouldn't expect him to be at work in; to see the breadth of the people that God is inviting into his new family.

Diversity within the New Testament – in Acts

Luke's focus on the diversity of the children of God is continued in his second volume, the book of Acts. The whole book is organised around the consequence of receiving the

---

13. Andy McCullough, *Made Flesh: John's Gospel, Mission and the Global Church* (Malcolm Down Publishing, 2024), Kindle edition, pp. 68-69.

Spirit in the very first chapter. 'But you will receive power when the Holy Spirit comes on you; and you will be my witnesses in Jerusalem, and in all Judea and Samaria, and to the ends of the earth' (Acts 1:8).

The rest of the book describes this happening, climaxing with the gospel reaching the ends of the known world, Rome. In the meantime, we see it spreading from Jerusalem to Judea and Samaria. Too often we can focus and desire the power element of the Spirit and forget the purpose of receiving the Spirit's power is to be witnesses to people like us (our Jerusalem), people we are comfortable with (our Judea), people who are geographically close to us but very different, even despised (our Samaria) and then to everyone (the ends of the earth). The book of Acts is written to describe the formation of the church; it describes the formation of a diverse church.

However, despite Jesus making it clear what the purpose of the coming of the Spirit was, it took a long time for that to happen; commentators suggest around a decade before the gospel is witnessed beyond Jerusalem. Within the structure of the book the catalyst for this is the speech given by Stephen in Acts 7.

Stephen's speech in Act 7

Stephen is brought before the Sanhedrin following false accusations made against him because he was having such an impact through the miraculous signs and the wisdom with which he argued (Acts 6:8-10). I find it fascinating that his response is to give a brief history of the people of Israel which doesn't seem to answer the accusations being made against him. What Stephen does do is:

> He consistently highlights the dynamic presence of God with his people outside the holy place (temple), city (Jerusalem) and land (Israel) and ultimately casts the temple as a 'hand-made' human creation (on a par with the golden calf!) where the Most High God most certainly 'does not dwell'.[14]

Stephen reminds his audience that God has always worked outside of Israel. For example, God spoke to Abraham while he was living in Mesopotamia (v. 2); it was later that he came to the land in which they are 'now living' (v. 4) but had no inheritance there. He talks about the goal of the Exodus was that they would leave captivity to 'worship me in this place' (v. 7). This place, as described in Exodus 3:12, is Mount Sinai, not the temple in Jerusalem. It is also mentioned in verses 6 and 7 that Abraham's descendants lived as resident aliens in other people's land for 400 years before entering the promised land.

Stephen then describes the story of Joseph in Egypt, with wandering becoming a way of life for the people of God. It also shows how Joseph's special gifts and calling were recognised by Pharoah, a foreign leader. Contrasting maybe with how Stephen's gifts are not being recognised by the Jerusalem council!

---

14. F. Scott Spencer, *Acts* (Sheffield: Sheffield Academic Press, 1997), p. 81.

The next larger section covers the ministry of Moses, verses 20-44. We see again the care for the people of God outside of the land of Israel. Moses encounters God in the burning bush (v. 30), which is 'holy ground' (v. 33) but is outside of the promised land. Miracles are performed, again outside the promised land (v. 36).

The theme of the rejection of Moses by his own people (vv. 21,27-28, 35, 39-41), is parallel to the rejection of both Stephen and Jesus.

The final section of the speech indicates the importance of the nomadic tabernacle that travelled with the people of God and remained with them in the promised land (vv. 45-50). The temple replaced the tabernacle, but Stephen emphasises that 'the Most High does not live in houses made by human hands' (v. 48). He then gives scriptural back-up to this claim in verses 49-50.

At the conclusion of the speech, Stephen is stoned and significantly we are told that 'Saul was there, giving approval to his death' (Acts 8:1, NIV 1984).

Following Stephen's speech, the believers witness to Jesus outside of Jerusalem

It took a decade but following Stephen's speech we see the gospel spreading outside of Jerusalem. The initial cause is persecution (8:1,4) with Philip taking a lead. The apostles then get involved in 8:14. We start to see the prophecy of Jesus from Acts 1:8 beginning to be fulfilled with witness taking place in Judea and Samaria. Luke makes the point that then the church throughout Judea, Galilee and Samaria 'enjoyed a time of peace. It was strengthened; and encouraged by the Holy Spirit, it grew in numbers, living in the fear of the Lord' (9:31, NIV 1984).

In chapter 9, Saul/Paul is then converted and receives a specific calling to take the gospel to the ends of the earth. Peter also receives his own 'conversion experience' in chapter 10 which frees him to share the gospel with Cornelius, a Roman centurion; the Spirit falls on him and all his household. In chapter 11 we have a truly diverse church established in Antioch, from which Paul and Barnabas are sent to establish other diverse churches across the Roman Empire (chapter 13 onwards).

Diversity isn't without its difficulties, with the major issue being how do the new converts relate to Judaism? This is worked out at the council of Jerusalem and is recorded in chapter 15. After this the witness truly does spread to the ends of the earth.

Most of Paul's letters deal with the challenges the early church faced in creating diverse churches and implementing the decision made at the council of Jerusalem. Life would have been so much easier if the council of Jerusalem had reached a different conclusion. Either that separate Jewish and Gentile churches should be established with their own unique characteristics, valuing diversity over unity; or for a single church to be established where Gentiles adopted Jewish culture, valuing unity over diversity. If these alternatives had been adopted, most of Paul's letters would not have needed writing.

The vision of the future

At the very end of the New Testament we have the book of Revelation, written to churches amid persecution to give them a vision of where things are heading, the New Jerusalem, to enable them to persevere. We are told that the New Jerusalem will be enriched because 'the glory and honour of the nations will be brought into it' (Revelation 21:26). Every culture and ethnicity will add to the splendour.

Our resurrection bodies will bring with them much of our old selves into the new creation. As the resurrected body of Jesus was both different yet recognisable, so will ours. Our resurrected bodies will keep our ethnicities, we will not lose our cultural and ethnic distinctives. 'After this I looked, and there before me was a great multitude that no one could count, from every nation, tribe, people and language, standing before the throne and before the Lamb' (Revelation 7:9).

As Tim Keller says, 'Final redemption, then, does not erase racial and cultural difference. Different cultures have their own particular glories and splendours, analogous to the differing gifts of the body of Christ.'[15]

Conclusions

We see the clear direction throughout Scripture, of unity while valuing diversity, through the Tower of Babel, the calling of Abraham, the diversity of the people of God in the Old Testament. We see the same emphasis in the New

---

15. https://gospelinlife.com/article/the-bible-and-race/ (accessed 9.10.24).

Testament both through the Gospels and the Acts of the apostles, with the church to be witnesses to Judea, Samaria, and the 'ends of the earth' (Acts 1:8), very similar to the original calling to Abraham.

Despite this clarity there is resistance – the message of Jesus in the Gospels of the diverse nature of the kingdom of God is a challenge to the perceived wisdom of the time. Despite the very definite words from the ascending Jesus, the early church took a decade to move beyond Jerusalem – only then because of persecution, insights from the soon-to-be-martyred Stephen and direct intervention from God. Before Cornelius could be converted, Peter needed to be converted.

It is not surprising that the church throughout the ages has had the same challenges, resisting the call to diversification, like the early church missing the clear commandment of Scripture. We send missionaries across oceans but fail to reach out to our neighbours who are different from us. Praying for revival but not seeing God answering those prayers by Christians from across the globe arriving on our shores to build up the church with their insights and vitality, to help us in our mission field.

It is hard to conclude anything other than God wants a united church that values and celebrates all the diverse backgrounds and cultures of those who are part of it; that he is calling us to journey towards it, whatever challenges and difficulties it causes.

Questions to ponder

- If the clear teaching of Scripture is that God values diversity and wants unity out of diversity, how much of a priority should it be for us? Are there other things that should have a higher priority for us?

- What do you think stops us from seeing the call of God to value diversity and implementing actions that support this in our lives and churches?

- What forces are at work in your context driving you towards uniformity?

2.

The Challenges the Early Church Faced: Antioch

I have already quoted ninety-year-old civil rights leader John Perkins who said, 'There is no institution on earth more equipped and capable of bringing transformation to the cause of reconciliation than the church. But we have some hard work to do.'[16]

Perkins was the son of sharecroppers, what slaves in the United States were called when they were released from slavery. He fled from the South as a young teenager when his brother was killed by a policeman. He became a Christian through the influence of his son who insisted they went to church. He subsequently wrote about his journey of reconciliation, forgiving and trusting white policemen and urging others into reconciliation. He gave the rest of his life to the work of racial reconciliation. It is well worth reading his books and watching his various talks, available on YouTube.

---

16. Perkins, *One Blood*, p. 63.

More recently, following George Floyd's death, the subsequent outpouring of emotion showed a desire for racial reconciliation, but also how ill-equipped the world is to achieve it. The Black Lives Matter (BLM) movement while powerful and important has in some cases led to increased polarisation and division. It even seems that many have given up on even trying to make a difference, maybe feeling the whole area is a minefield and sensing a lack of ability to navigate it. We have seen that the biblical calling of the church is unity while valuing diversity. However, I believe that we, the church, have abdicated from the role of modelling how people from diverse backgrounds live healthily together, leaving the world to inadequately try to fill the void.

In this chapter we will be looking at the experience of the early church to help us understand why racial reconciliation is difficult, and what it is that makes it hard. Having looked at the obstacles, we can then see how we can overcome them. The world desperately needs the church to step up to play its role in racial reconciliation, a role multicultural churches are uniquely equipped to do.

We have already seen something of the journey in the early chapters of Acts towards the first Gentile converts. For the first decade or more of its life, the church was monocultural, a Jewish-only entity. This is despite what happened on the day of Pentecost when everyone miraculously heard the gospel in their own languages, and the prophecy from Jesus that the church should be witnesses to Samaria, Judea and to the 'ends of the earth' (Acts 1:8).

Then Peter had a vision from God, repeated three times, that leads him to the first Gentile convert, Cornelius. It was fully orchestrated by God. For Cornelius to find faith, Peter had to be convinced that it was possible, and it was what God intended. He needed a paradigm shift in his thinking. God broke in and spoke into the situation. That is the essence of Acts 10. Before Cornelius could be converted, Peter had to be converted to a new way of thinking.

Then in the next chapter we read:

> Now those who had been scattered by the persecution that broke out when Stephen was killed travelled as far as Phoenicia, Cyprus and Antioch, spreading the word only among Jews. Some of them, however, men from Cyprus and Cyrene, went to Antioch and began to speak to Greeks also, telling them the good news about the Lord Jesus. The Lord's hand was with them, and a great number of people believed and turned to the Lord.
>
> *(Acts 11:19-21)*

It took time, but once Peter had his mind changed, which led to the first Gentile convert, the floodgates were opened to many more. Again, to note, it was the result of persecution, it wasn't planned by man but orchestrated by God. This led to the church in Antioch being the first truly multicultural church, the first reconciled church with Jew and Gentile in true and full community together. A couple of chapters on we are introduced to the leadership of the Antioch church.

Acts 13:1: 'Now in the church at Antioch there were prophets and teachers: Barnabas, Simeon called Niger, Lucius of Cyrene, Manaen (who had been brought up with Herod the tetrarch) and Saul.'

We see the diversity of Antioch not just in community but in church leadership:

Name	Origin	Ethnicity	Other detail
Barnabas	Cyprus	Greek Jew	Rich – sold fields
Simeon (Niger)	Unknown	Black	
Lucius	Cyrene	African	
Manaen	Palestinian	Greek, Herodian	Wealthy aristocrat
Saul	Tarsus/ Jerusalem	Hebrew Jew	Pharisee

This truly ethnically diverse church sent Saul and Barnabas out across the Mediterranean world to share the truth to people from many different diverse backgrounds.

> From Attalia they sailed back to Antioch, where they had been committed to the grace of God for the work they had now completed. On arriving there, they gathered the church together and reported all that God had done through them and how he had opened a door of faith to the Gentiles.
>
> *(Acts 14:26-27)*

It is not surprising that the DNA at the heart of the church in Antioch went with Paul and Barnabas as they travelled around, starting churches that reflected the diversity of the mother church in Antioch.

Also, unsurprisingly, the church in Antioch has been raised up as the model for diverse churches across the centuries. The church in Antioch is a great encouragement to those of us who want to follow a model of a multicultural church.

However, that is not the full story. It does not help us understand why we have hard work to do.

What we have seen so far makes the following scripture so shocking and unexpected. This is Paul, one of the original leaders of the church in Antioch, talking to the churches in Galatia about something that happened in the Antioch church. Cephas is the Aramaic form of the Greek name Peter. Paul is emphasising the Hebrew background of Peter.

> When Cephas came to Antioch, I opposed him to his face, because he stood condemned. For before certain men came from James, he used to eat with the Gentiles. But when they arrived, he began to draw back and separate himself from the Gentiles because he was afraid of those who belonged to the circumcision group. The other Jews joined him in his hypocrisy, so that by their hypocrisy even Barnabas was led astray. When I saw that they were not acting in line with the truth of the gospel, I said to Cephas in front of them all, 'You are a Jew, yet you live like a Gentile and not like a Jew. How is it, then, that you force Gentiles to follow Jewish customs?'
>
> *(Galatians 2:11-14)*

Diversity had been laid into the foundations of the church, the very DNA of the church in Antioch, and so it is not a surprise to find everyone eating together. Eating together was at the heart of fellowship, at the heart of relationships then, as it is in most cultures today. So, their oneness in Christ was expressed in having meals together, bridging differences and diversity.

As an aside, I would encourage you to consider having meals with people from other cultures if you are not already doing so. I have observed that many churches with people from different nations will have communal meals together, with people bringing their own nation's meals. They are great times. However great that is, eating in each other's homes goes far beyond that and strengthens relationships across boundaries like nothing else can.

The foundations in Antioch, which treated everyone as equal, including everyone eating together, were shattered. Paul saw this as a total denial of the gospel which says we are all equal, 'all one in Christ Jesus' (Galatians 3:28), and he challenged Peter to his face. He was also willing to go public about it, writing to these churches in Galatia about the incident because he saw it as being so fundamental.

Tim Keller explains Paul's argument, 'God didn't have fellowship with you based on your ethnicity or culture. How can you therefore have fellowship with others on that basis?'[17]

Paul isn't just saying racism is a sin, he is identifying the roots of racism, as a denial of the gospel, putting works alongside faith. He is not just calling for repentance of the sin of racism but 'repent of the sin of forgetting your

---

17. https://gospelinlife.com/article/the-bible-and-race/ (accessed 9.10.24).

gracious welcome by God through the costly sacrifice of Christ'.[18] It is not the behaviours that Paul focuses on but the self-righteousness that lies behind it. He is using grace as a motivator to a change of behaviour.

We need to recognise that if this could happen in the model diverse church in Antioch, no wonder John Perkins says there is hard work to do.

The question we must ask is, how on earth did it happen? If it can happen in Antioch, a church that had diverse leadership, a church that sent Paul and Barnabas to reach Gentiles, it can happen anywhere. If Peter, who had a vision from God that led to him preaching to Cornelius and declaring that God had shown him that he should not call anyone 'impure or unclean' (Acts 10), could go astray, any one of us is vulnerable. If Peter, who convinced everyone else that the separation between Jew and Gentile had been broken, could end up separating himself from Gentiles, then anyone can fall. Anyone includes you and me.

We have hard work to do.

Why do you think it happened?

I must admit it is only very recently that my attention was drawn to this. I knew about what Paul said in Galatians but had not registered it was in the diverse church in Antioch that the incident took place. I have been forced to ask the questions, why did Peter and Barnabas and the other Jews separate out? Why did the Gentiles allow it? Important questions if we are going to understand the hard work we

---

18. https://gospelinlife.com/article/the-bible-and-race/ (accessed 9.10.24).

must do if we are going to build churches that truly reflect the gospel mandate of unity while celebrating diversity, churches that will then be able to contribute to bringing racial reconciliation to the world.

I struggled long and hard to understand and have concluded there were at least two reasons, one mentioned in the text itself, the other something we can deduce. I think both are relevant to us today. They both need to be overcome if we are to be successful in our mission to build churches that reflect the kingdom of God and can influence society.

The impact of fear

Firstly, Paul says they were 'afraid' (Galatians 2:12). Fear of what people think can play a significant role in racism. Let us not underestimate the impact of what others think. Why don't we speak out when people are being racist? It is not easy to call people out without being seen to be rude or judgemental. My parents regularly spoke about foreigners in derogatory terms. I struggled with it but failed to confront them appropriately. What stopped me? Fear. Fear of getting it wrong, fear of what they would think of me. Recently I have made a definite decision that when I am confronted with racism I will try to always speak out in as loving and caring way as possible, not allowing fear to stop me from confronting racism.

Fear is such a powerful force. It can stop us stepping out and doing something different even if we want to. The fear of what others think stops us from doing things that go against the consensus. Fear is a factor now as then.

There are so many other examples of the impact of fear. There can also be a real or imagined expectation that we will worship within our own communities. When British people live abroad it is expected that they will worship in an English church. Having worked a little with churches in Spain I have seen very few English people worshipping other than in English churches. Similarly, here in the UK there is sometimes an expectation that worshippers will go to a church based on their culture. Many Nigerians from the Yorùbá tribe worship within the Redeemed Christian Church of God churches. It takes courage and strength to stand against this. I am in awe of those families that worship with us rather than another church in Luton that reflects their ethnic background. They tell me of the very real pressure they feel to conform; it was an even greater challenge for the first few people that made a conscious decision to worship in a predominantly white church. Even if people want to worship in a mixed congregation, the fear of what others think can stop them. If you are white, ask yourself what people would think if you started worshipping in a black majority church.

There was fear that stopped me confronting my parents' racist attitudes, but also a sense that I didn't have the energy to keep fighting the battle with them. Overcoming our fears takes energy; the two are very closely related. The same is true in so many areas. It takes energy to speak up for refugees, many of whom have paid a great price to come to our country, leaving family and friends to be treated very badly when they get here. Yes, some are economic refugees, but most are not, as demonstrated by the large numbers who apply for the right to remain and are granted it. It takes energy to keep challenging the prejudice and misunderstandings.

Or energy to confront the deep-seated assumption that immigration from the white empire is somehow different from people of colour coming to our country. I don't always have energy to challenge misogynist attitudes that devalue women. Deep-seated injustices and prejudices take energy to keep confronting. It is even more challenging for those who are the victims of such prejudice, so many give up fighting.

However, it is worth noting as an aside that fear of what others think can be used to a positive end. One of the positive things that came out of the BLM movement was that overt racism became less socially acceptable, for example, at football matches. With teams taking the knee before kick-off and various other initiatives to kick racism out of football, there is now significantly less racism on the terraces in the UK game. The change has been so profound that when our teams play overseas, they are sometimes horrified by the racism they face.

In addition to the fear of what others think, there is also a genuine fear of being in a new situation with people who are different from us, fear of saying the wrong thing, and doing the wrong thing. We like to feel at home, safe, feeling that we fit in. In new situations, with new people, especially if they are different from us, there is the fear of embarrassing ourselves and others. This has happened to me so many times! I remember my first visit to a church in Spain; the leaders picked a colleague and me up from the airport and took us to their home and offered us some food. I thought it was a little early for lunch but was hungry after the flight, so got stuck in and enjoyed a good meal. It was therefore a big surprise when we were taken out for lunch! Unknown to me, what I had been offered at the home was 'second breakfast'. The hosts were surprised I ate so much; I was embarrassed.

One time, soon after arriving in a new town, we were invited to a neighbour's barbecue; we hardly knew them and saw this as a perfect opportunity to get to know them better and probably others in the street. Living next door, we could see all the preparations taking place and were really looking forward to it. However, late in the morning guests started to arrive, but our invitation said 2 p.m. What could we do? We kept looking out the bedroom window and everyone seemed to be having a good time, but they were very early. Should we just turn up and ignore the time on the invitation? In the end we decided to wait until 2 p.m. and see what happened. Come 2 p.m., nothing changed. By 2.30 p.m. we decided we had to do something, so went round ready to make a quick getaway if we had got it wrong. We were warmly welcomed by the hosts. Within the next ten minutes many more new people turned up. What had happened was that family were invited at 10 a.m. for lunch together before neighbours joined at 2 p.m. Clearly other neighbours were as uncertain as us, so too had been watching to see what was happening. When they saw us arrive and be welcomed, they were empowered to join us. This new, uncertain situation within my own culture provoked fear of getting it wrong, even though I had been praying that God would use it to build relationships with our new neighbours. As a postscript to the story, before we had moved to another town our neighbours had come to Christ and become key parts of the church.

Therefore, when inviting people from different cultures to us for meals or events, we must overcome our own fear of what to eat, what the expectations are. We also need to be aware that our guests will be having to overcome their fears. 'Perfect love drives out fear' (1 John 4:18). We need to enable our experience of the love of Christ to produce a love of other people who Christ loves. It is that love that enables us to overcome our fear and enables us to build multicultural churches that impact the world. It is that love that enables us to look beyond our feelings to be able to focus our concern on how others are feeling.

The impact of deeply ingrained societal norms

Secondly, in Antioch I think the idea of the separation between Jews and Gentiles was so deeply ingrained that it was just expected in society as a whole and that influenced the church. We must recognise that the church is always influenced by the society it is part of. Not all the influences are bad, but we must discern the negative impacts. The church is meant to impact the world, to be salt and light in the world (Matthew 5:13-14). We must resist the pressures from the world to squeeze us into its mould. That, I believe, was happening here. The initial impact of the gospel of unity amid diversity caused Jews and Gentiles to eat together. This was radical, and a powerful statement to the surrounding society. It was totally countercultural. It was a sign of the kingdom of God breaking in. However, it was fragile and easily lost. People, including Peter and Barnabas, when the pressure was on quickly reverted to what they knew. They probably did it without much intentional thought, shocking as it may seem to us looking back.

The issue was not just separation; within the separation was the idea of Jewish superiority and Gentile inferiority that had been deeply ingrained for generations. It became automatic and hard to break. Jews just saw themselves as superior, Gentiles inferior. I suggest that fear of the disapproval of their peers mostly explained why the Jews separated themselves out. I suggest expectations and feelings of superiority and inferiority explains why Gentiles, including Gentile leaders, allowed it to happen. These ingrained expectations were so strong within them that they had lost the energy to fight for the truth of all being one in Christ. It may have been the reason why they went along with it, Gentiles wearily accepting their status as second-class citizens.

Thank God for Paul who saw through it and challenged it as a denial of the gospel. Challenged it then and by writing about it, challenges it now and forever. Sometimes it is someone coming into a situation with fresh eyes who can see ungodly practices.

This helps me grasp why we have such hard work to do. It is not just fear of what others think; racial prejudice or racial preference is so deeply rooted in all of us, white and non-white. Sometimes it is so deeply rooted we do not even see it, or if we see it, we don't have the energy to fight it.

These truths are not just relevant regarding ethnicity, they are also true with regards to social class. In many cultures, certainly in the UK, there are deep divisions and misunderstandings between working and middle-class cultures. A divide between us and the bosses, a divide between shop floor and management.

We need to acknowledge that if it can happen in a diverse church, with diverse leadership like in Antioch, if it can happen to senior, experienced leaders like Peter and Barnabas, it can happen anywhere. It can happen here with us.

We need to be open to the impact of fear of what others think. We also need to be open to the impact of deeply ingrained assumptions of superiority and inferiority that have been there for generations.

We can so easily settle for behaviour and habits that are not helpful. Our behaviour can be based on generations of assumptions which we never consciously consider. To change we must be persistently intentional. We must form new habits that mirror our values. This takes time and determination, or we can make short-term gestures but end up with our default and expect everyone to fit in with that.

We need to deal with these things as individuals, and as churches, and then we can play our role in bringing racial reconciliation in society. We do have the advantage of the Spirit of unity living within us, but it doesn't mean it is easy.

A few further thoughts on what breaking societal norms means in practice

Isaiah described a picture God had given him of the age to come:

> The wolf will live with the lamb, the leopard will lie down with the goat, the calf and the lion and the yearling together; and a little child will lead them.
>
> *(Isaiah 11:6; see also Isaiah 65:25)*

The image of the wolf living peacefully with the lamb looks very different from the perspective of the wolf from that of the lamb. The wolf needs to give up its instinct to feel superior to the lamb, give up its power over the lamb. The lamb needs to learn to trust the wolf. Both need to overcome their natural instincts. It is costly to both, but in very different ways. It is a very helpful picture to keep in mind as we seek to overcome the obstacles and challenges to building multicultural churches.

This is an insightful observation recorded by Tom Wright:

> I was at a conference in America talking about Paul's vision for the church in which there was 'neither Jew nor Greek, slave nor free, no male and female'. I was stopped in my tracks by a sympathetic but sharp-minded critic, an African American woman theologian whose own book on Paul I much appreciated. 'You need to remember,' she said to me, 'that when you talk about being "all one in Christ Jesus", what people like me hear – whether you mean it like that or not – is that "you are all now welcome to become honorary white males".' Ouch.[19]

Quite possibly both Tom Wright and his African American theologian friend need to change; Tom being clearer in what he is saying, his friend in what she instinctively hears.

Research looking at multiracial churches in the USA was discussed in an article in *Christianity Today*. The research found most of these churches tended to mimic white culture

---

19. https://ntwrightpage.com/2020/06/14/undermining-racism-complete-text/ (accessed 9.10.24). Permission received.

and theology. It found that white people struggle with black church culture and are unwilling to embrace any form of black church culture. Therefore, multiracial churches remain diverse to the extent that white members feel comfortable.[20]

I am aware of this happening within UK churches. I have many non-white friends who have been instrumental in helping predominantly white churches become multiracial. The challenge they faced was not increasing the diversity within the congregation, but was changing the values and culture of the churches to incorporate aspects of non-white cultures. It was as if the barriers between Jews and Gentiles, black and white had been broken down so that everyone could be white.

In Bible times the assumption for generations was of the superiority of Jewish culture, that others needed to fit in with the Jewish way of doing things. Now it is the superiority of white culture that we must be aware of.

The white wolf needs to be willing to give up some things to fully fellowship with the lamb. We all need to die to our previous self and become a new person in Christ. In every context the majority culture must learn to listen to and be willing to be influenced by the minority culture. The minority culture people must learn how to trust majority culture people. This is especially difficult if the minority culture people are carrying wounds from the past.

A friend who leads a majority Jamaican church shared with me that many in his church questioned whether a white person worshipping in a majority white church could truly be a Christian because of their experience of racism. We

---

20. www.christianitytoday.com/2021/02/race-diversity-multiethnic-church-movement-promise/ (accessed 9.10.24).

are working together to try to break that stereotype. He has also talked to me of the challenges faced not just within his congregation but his black denomination, of integrating white people without them just becoming leaders by default, as that is everyone's expectation – white people that they will lead, black people that they will be led.

There is hard work for us to do if we are wanting to be part of the type of churches Jesus envisaged, churches that demonstrate the kingdom of God, that celebrate unity and diversity. Churches that will then influence the world for good.

Do you, like me, want to be in a church where all backgrounds are equally recognised and valued? We must recognise it is easier said than done. This is the hard work we must do before we can help the world. As in Antioch, prejudice is deeply ingrained, expectations are deeply ingrained; often we do not even know they are there. We must move beyond celebrating diversity for diversity's sake. We must challenge racial attitudes that reinforce systemic inequality. The research published in *Christianity Today* suggested that in the USA that is not happening despite the number of multiracial churches growing. People of colour in such churches are often relegated to symbolic roles that people see – ushers, singers – but have no real influence or authority in the church. This even happens when racially homogenous churches merge to become a racially diverse church. Over time white people end up occupying the roles with greatest authority.

These are the findings of research in the USA; it is also the experience of many of my non-white friends seeking to serve the UK church.

We need to be open to expect and desire everyone to play a part, to take responsibility. Whether white or black, majority or minority, wolf or lamb, to make the adjustments in our thinking and practice required to bring unity while not destroying diversity.

We must allow all different cultures to express themselves, not impose our culture onto others, or discard our culture in favour of another.

Questions to ponder

- Reflect on times that you have stayed quiet in the face of prejudice. Why was that? Fear of what others might think? Lack of energy?

- Have you ever experienced a situation where you felt you didn't fit? How hard was this to overcome? What enabled you to persevere, assuming you did?

- Are you convinced that the church has a contribution to make towards racial reconciliation? If so, how can we make a difference to society? To what extent do fear and ingrained expectations prevent this happening? How can we work to overcome them?

3.

The Impact of Prejudice

We have looked at what the Bible says about unity and diversity. We have also looked at how we are challenged to play our part in the racial reconciliation; to be a light to the world. We have also seen that there are obstacles to overcome before we can do this. In this chapter, I want to turn up the heat a little and bluntly state that prejudice generally, and racism specifically, is sinful, it is wrong. It is an obstacle that needs to be acknowledged and overcome. Many of the themes we will look at have already been alluded to; however, there is a power in looking at them altogether to motivate us to change. All Christians should acknowledge that prejudice is wrong and then seek to repent of it as it falls short of the glory of God (Romans 3:23).

The image of God
At the very heart of the revelation from God is the acknowledgement that all humans have equal dignity and worth as persons created in the image of God (Genesis

1:26-28). Everyone, whatever our ethnicity, social position or gender, has equal dignity and worth because we are created in the image of God. However, we can deny this in both thought and action, as James tells us in his letter: 'With the tongue we praise our Lord and Father, and with it we curse human beings, who have been made in God's likeness' (James 3:9).

To address someone without respect violates the image of God. 'It is a sin to treat any class or group unequally, as being less worthy of respect, love and protection.'[21]

God himself is no respecter of persons, whatever ethnicity, or social status, or gender you are. This is clear from just two of a multitude of scriptures.

> For the LORD your God is God of gods and Lord of lords, the great God, mighty and awesome, who shows no partiality and accepts no bribes. He defends the cause of the fatherless and the widow, and loves the foreigner residing aong you, giving them food and clothing.
> *(Deuteronomy 10:17-18)*

> Then Peter began to speak: 'I now realise how true it is that God does not show favouritism but accepts from every nation the one who fears him and does what is right.'
> *(Acts 10:34-35)*

Discrimination and favouritism fall short of both God's glory and his character.

---

21. https://quarterly.gospelinlife.com/the-sin-of-racism/ (accessed 9.10.24).

The great commandment – to love your neighbour as yourself

When challenged to identify the greatest commandment, Jesus summarises the law of God in two great commandments. To 'Love the Lord your God with all your heart and with all your soul and with all your mind ... And the second is like it: "Love your neighbour as yourself"' (Matthew 22:36-40).

When asked to define love for our neighbour in Luke 10:25-37, in the parable of the good Samaritan Jesus describes someone who makes great sacrifices and takes significant risks to meet the physical and material needs of someone who is from a different ethnicity and religion than themself. When we read the parable, we often see ourselves as the Samaritan. However, maybe a better understanding has Jesus as the Samaritan, and us as the injured man. Jesus is the one who pays the cost, who makes the sacrifice on our behalf.

At the end of the parable, we are told to 'do likewise', to follow the attitude and actions of Jesus towards us with regards to others. To treat people of other ethnicities, classes and groups with the same care, respect and love that Jesus has shown towards us and we show to people within our own community. By implication, failure to do so is to disobey the greatest commandment.

The new creation

Jesus' death and resurrection inaugurated a new creation. Jesus rose as the first fruits of the age to come (1 Corinthians 15:20-23). The Holy Spirit has been given to us as a downpayment, a deposit of the future renewed world bursting into the present (Ephesians 1:14-16). We are united to a future world where there will be no more suffering, tears, injustice, evil and sin. This new world is partially with us now. It is breaking into the present. One of the marks of this new world, this new creation, is the end of all ethnic and national strife, alienation and violence. An end of all class and gender battles. As we have seen, the book of Revelation describes a future of all the people of God, from every tongue, tribe, people and nation worshipping together (Revelation 7:9).

Our distinctives will be carried over into the new creation, but sinful distortions will be done away with. We are called to bear witness to the future glory in our lives in the present. Treating people differently based on ethnicity, social class or gender is a denial of this (Galatians 3:26-28).

The gospel of faith alone

There is something within all of us that likes to think we have earned and deserved what we have received. We would rather see ourselves as the deserving head boy or girl rather than as dirty rotten sinners. In doing so we rely on our achievements and pedigree for our significance and security. This can create a real sense of insecurity because deep down we know that we are not the good, loveable, worthy people we would want to be.

It is to bolster our own sense of self-worth that we look down on other cultures and ethnicities. We have a need to see ourselves as the good ones in contrast to others. Our cultural preferences become moral absolutes and badges of honour.

This influences how we view and value church practices. For example, what level of emotion is appropriate, musical style, length of service become elevated in importance more than they should. We see our practices as superior to others; we can even perceive them as more pleasing to God.

We break this by a full understanding of the gospel of grace, the truth that we are saved by grace alone, not based on any outward signs. The outward signs are not what is important, yet too easily they do become important, therefore denying the gospel.

Ironically it is possible to denounce racists and have a sense of being morally superior to them! In doing so, we lose sight of the reality of common fallen humanity! The reality is that we are all sinners and are vulnerable to prejudice. Denouncing others therefore can just aggravate our divisions.

Corporate and individual racism

Clearly it is possible for individuals to be racist, but there is resistance within some church contexts to the possibility of the existence of systemic or structural racism and prejudice generally. I have read so much that denies structural prejudice exists, and had many discussions with friends who deny it, saying it is just part of the 'woke' agenda.

I suggest that there are social structures supported by the dominant racial group that excludes and oppresses racial minorities. These structures can be sustained by individuals who do not themselves hold or practise racist views and behaviours. This is structural racism, and we all bear corporate guilt and responsibility for not working to dismantle these oppressive structures.

The Bible clearly talks about both individual and corporate sin, guilt and responsibility. Daniel repented of the sin of his ancestors in Daniel 9. Achan's family were implicated in his sin; they had to bear guilt for their impact on his character (Joshua 7).

Proverbs talks about the impact of our decisions as individuals but also recognises that injustice and poverty are not just the result of the individual choices we make, but can be the result of social structures – see for example Proverbs 13:23: 'An unploughed field produces food for the poor, but injustice sweeps it away.'

Therefore, let us not dismiss too easily the possibility of corporate sin alongside individuals sinning.

How we might be sinning

I have learned that I am not always aware of when I am sinning! I am aware of my general sinfulness but looking back at my life, I can now see things I have done, or not done, said, or not said, that I am now horrified at. I guess the same is true for all of us. Therefore, before leaving this subject of sin, let us look at ways we might be sinning but are unaware of.

We can be sinning by not doing anything to combat racism

Tom Wright says: 'Let me be blunt. It simply won't do merely to say, "Racism is sinful and we must get rid of it." The churches worldwide have known that for a long time and it's had little effect.'[22] He goes on to say:

> What we now call 'racism' is not simply, for Christians, a failure to obey one or other moral standard – e.g. that we should love our neighbour as ourselves. It is deeper even than that. It is a failure of vocation . . . Rejecting racism and embracing the diversity of Jesus' family ought to be as obvious as praying the Lord's Prayer, celebrating the Eucharist, or reading the four Gospels. It isn't just an extra 'rule' we're supposed to keep. It is constitutive of who we are.

We need to be honest about the problems faced not just in society, but also in the church, and we need to seek to do something about it. As Tom Wright says, 'it is not enough to say the right things, we need to be doing something'. Doing something as individuals and as the church. We need to be acting if necessary to combat racism in the church as well as in society. Otherwise, I think we are guilty of sin.

We can have a too simplistic view of racism

We need to see beyond a simplistic definition of racism as intentional acts of racial discrimination by immoral individuals. We need to see beyond the simple idea of prejudice as a good/bad binary, with prejudice a terrible evil. Such a view can cause us to deny its reality. If we have a good/bad binary to say white people are prejudiced it implies they are bad,

---

22. https://ntwrightpage.com/2020/06/14/undermining-racism-complete-text/ (accessed 9.10.24). Permission received.

which we don't want to do, therefore we don't admit white people are prejudiced. (Obviously it is not just white people who can be prejudiced, but I write as a white man.)

We need to recognise that prejudice is everywhere. Those who are the victims don't find it difficult to see prejudice all around them, but may not see it within themselves! White people, or those with social power, may struggle to see it at all. The truth is there is a continuum of racism and prejudice, and we are all guilty at some level.

Even recently my prejudice was exposed in the way that I used humour which reinforced unhelpful stereotypes. I often post light-hearted humour on social media as well as more serious context. It is good to have a laugh, as demonstrated by the fact that my jokes are much more popular than any of my serious content. I posted a joke that I thought was witty and clever. I had copied it from elsewhere because I enjoyed it. I am even tempted to share it now so you can have a laugh! However, someone close to me challenged me about it. Others had spoken to them saying they thought the joke was offensive but didn't feel able to challenge me. My close friend did challenge me. On first look I found it hard to see why it was offensive and prejudiced rather than just funny. I therefore initially stood my ground. Which made its own point. I am not the best judge of how others view things. I asked my wife for her opinion, knowing she would be honest with me, and feeling sure she would support me. She was shocked that I could be so unaware and foolish to not see the offence, and expressed it in a way that only wives can. At that point I knew I needed to take the post down and offer apologies. We can all be prejudiced and totally blind to it.

We therefore must be willing to be called out on it without taking offence or feeling we are a bad person.

Other ways we can avoid recognising racism

We can avoid action by declaring ourselves to be colourblind. The number of times I have heard white people justify their position on ethnicity by declaring they are colourblind when it comes to how they view people! This phrase comes from a Martin Luther King speech where he shares his dream that people will not be judged by the colour of their skin but by the content of their character.[23] That is certainly a future that I too long for. However, in our current world the dream is not yet a reality. This, therefore, becomes a simple and convenient way to ignore racial issues. While in most cases it is well intentioned, in practice it serves to deny racism exists, which it surely does, and stops us doing anything about it. The reality is that white solidarity protects advantages and protects white people who feel racial discomfort. Too often we keep a benign silence and don't even admit our advantages. I don't think we can justify being colourblind just yet.

Another way I see people avoiding action is by declaring and labelling any discussions about racism and prejudice to be part of a 'woke' agenda. One of the most popular books challenging white people to see how they can be racist without being aware of it is *White Fragility* by Robin DiAngelo. It does not claim to be a 'Christian' book, and I have no idea of Robin's faith background. What horrifies me is the reaction to the book by so many Christian commentators. Many of

---

23. Speech given at the March on Washington for Jobs and Freedom on 28 August 1963.

them don't grapple with the case she makes but attack her personally and where she is coming from.[24]

I find Tim Keller helpful in addressing critical race theory and the 'woke' agenda.[25] He is willing to acknowledge where critical race theory is helpful while recognising it is incomplete. There are elements that are consistent with biblical truth, but we have much more to say on the subject.

The bottom line is that we should never dismiss something by giving it a label. In such a sensitive area as prejudice, we must consider Jesus' comment recorded in Matthew 7:3: 'Why do you look at the speck of sawdust in your brother's eye and pay no attention to the plank in your own eye?'

What is fascinating is that white people are more likely to choose segregation than other ethnicities. They expect racial comfort and are less tolerant of racial stress. I observe this in different forms. Luton has some of the highest achieving schools in the country; many are identified as outstanding by Ofsted. Due to the ethnic make-up of the town, white students are in the minority in our schools. I know of many families, including the families of church leaders, who either send their children to schools outside of the town which are not considered to be as academically good but are majority white, or move from Luton when their children get to a certain age for the sake of their education. I am not saying whether this is right or wrong, I just cite it as a symptom of white people being intolerant of racial stress and choosing segregation.

---

24. Robin DiAngelo, *White Fragility: Why It's So Hard for White People to Talk About Racism* (London: Penguin, 2019).
25. https://gospelinlife.com/article/a-biblical-critique-of-secular-justice-and-critical-theory/ (accessed 9.10.24).

I have also observed that white people, in the church as well as outside, tend to have strong opinions on race issues without necessarily understanding their complexity and devoting intentional time to studying the issues. I am so aware of how this applies to myself, and therefore the need for me to demonstrate humility and to listen to others and seek to grow in my personal understanding of the issues. Minorities live with injustice and prejudice all the time; they therefore can't help but be relative experts! As white people, we must work hard to understand the issues, but we are less motivated to do so and often don't spend the time and effort required. Yet we think we understand.

It is easy to have an individualistic worldview that doesn't have space to see the impact that race, class and gender have on opportunities that others are denied. We don't understand how our group identities are shaped by the media, schools, jokes and history. We can inadvertently end up protecting white advantage. The status quo is comfortable for white people, and we can't move things forward without becoming uncomfortable. This requires understanding and determination.

Looking in at a bird cage we may not see the confines that the bird has. We can be against racism, but still benefit from its benefits. White supremacy is an overarching system which is often invisible. White people still control many aspects of our society. It is important to name it. Too many white people are unaware of their privileges and the unequal playing field. For the most part, in the West we live in a segregated and unequal society. White people are not taught to see themselves in racial terms or draw attention to our race. We are born into a culture in which we belong – for example,

Western make-up is designed for white people. We therefore don't see race. When we get a job, it is because we deserve it, not because of our ethnicity. If others feel inferior that is their issue, nothing to do with me being superior. We are rarely even called white or think of ourselves as white.

For all these reasons we need to be constantly aware that we can be guilty of the sin of prejudice without recognising it. Having said all this, we also need to acknowledge that it is possible to see prejudice when it is not there. Life is never simple!

Seeing prejudice when it is not there

David Anderson introduces the concept of 'dotism' following a social experiment he came across.[26] Ten people were to be interviewed for a job. Before the interview a red dot was painted on one of their cheeks. After the interview, there was a debrief. Each of the ten said the interviewer kept staring at the red dot on their cheek. However, five didn't have a red dot – they had a clear one that couldn't be seen. Yet they still felt the interviewer was focusing on the dot! While prejudice does exist, it is also true that people feel self-conscious about whatever makes them insecure, or they feel makes them standout, for example, weight, gender, colour, any perceived negative distinctive.

It is obviously possible for people to feel they are being prejudiced against when they are not.

Even as a white male I have felt on occasions that I have been prejudiced against. Was it really a red dot moment, or

---

26. David A. Anderson, *Gracism: The Art of Inclusion* (Lisle, IL: IVP, 2007), p. 1.

was it just in my imagination? On one occasion I visited an adventure centre in Hong Kong while visiting my son who was working there for a season. The centre was mostly frequented by mainland Chinese tourists. All the men were smaller than me and wearing very similar suits. I was wearing shorts and felt everyone was focusing on my bare, long legs which seemed to stand out a mile! Were they looking or was I just imagining it?

I enjoy running – slower now than previously, but I still enjoy it. I remember running in an open athletic race; people were put into a heat based on their expected finishing time. Most of the others in my heat were teenage girls. I again felt conspicuous because I felt different from everyone else in the race. I have also been the only white person in a black church.

When we are in a situation where everyone is different from us, we can assume that others are focusing on our red dot. In all the incidents cited, that was my initial perception; I obviously could not know for sure and even if they were, I had no way of knowing what they were thinking.

My experience is nothing compared to that experienced by others – for example, regularly being stopped by the police or border control when entering their own country. So many of my friends tell me horrific stories of their experiences. They spend their whole lives conscious of the red dot on their cheek, and worse, the concern that their children have red dots! (Obviously the colour of a person's skin is undeniably a red dot.) Therefore, they have to give lectures to their children about what to do if stopped by people in authority, something I have never had to consider.

I have a Muslim friend who took his wife and young family on holiday to a bed and breakfast guest house by the coast.

My friend has a beard, and his wife wears a scarf to cover her hair rather than a hijab. When they arrived, they were told they were not welcome because of the concern that they might be terrorists and what neighbours would think if they were allowed to stay! My friend is very resilient, but I am sure this sort of experience must have an impact. It is therefore inevitable that there is the possibility of seeing prejudice even when it doesn't exist.

The other side of the story is that someone can be wrongly accused of prejudice. Once when working in industry, I interviewed two people for a job. I appointed the white guy rather than the Asian. Was I racist? Looking back, I honestly am not sure, but suspect there might have been some prejudice there. I suspect I might because at that time I knew few, if any, Asians, and there were not many in that workplace. Therefore, his ethnicity would have stood out like a red dot. However, did that prejudice my decision? The Asian guy may have felt I was prejudiced against him; he could have accused me of racism. I don't know how I would have felt if he had; my guess is I would have been very defensive and that might have easily transformed into aggression and self-justification. I know it would have been a very difficult exchange. I doubt if I would have been able to view the situation dispassionately.

Conclusion

Prejudice is clearly not just an important subject, it is an immotive subject, and it is highly complex. The way forward must be through humility, to listen to the perspective of others and seek wisdom from God. These are themes we look at later in the book.

What we shouldn't deny is that barriers exist between people; these barriers include prejudice. We need to be aware of these barriers and work to break them down if we are going to build an inclusive culture. We should never underestimate the complex challenges we face in doing so.

Questions to ponder

- How does seeing prejudice as a continuum and therefore something we are all guilty of, even if we are unaware of it, change our perspective?
- In what ways might you be guilty of prejudice?
- Why is not doing anything to combat racism and prejudice sinful?

4.

Principalities and Powers: Prejudice Viewed as Spiritual Warfare

We have looked at God's vision, as shared in Scripture, of a unified church that celebrates diversity in all forms and that reflects the reality of the age to come. We have seen the importance of churches that model this and are then able to begin to help the world as they too seek reconciliation in various forms. We have also looked at some of the challenges that need to be overcome if we are to achieve God's purposes, including the sin of prejudice. In this chapter we will focus on the work of our enemy, Satan, who seeks to undermine all God's objectives, including building churches that influence the world in bringing people from different backgrounds healthily together: 'For our struggle is not against flesh and blood, but against the rulers, against the authorities, against the powers of this dark world and against the spiritual forces of evil in the heavenly realms (Ephesians 6:12).

The subject of principalities and powers was clearly important and relevant for Paul and was regularly discussed in his letters.

Principalities and powers were also recognised in the early church. However, in recent times, the Western church has not given them much attention. We have given some thought to the general work of Satan, but not much to what Paul says about principalities and powers.

According to theologian Marva Dawn[27] we have lost focus on principalities and powers for two main reasons. During the period of the Reformation there were many extreme groups; these groups had an unhealthy over-fascination with principalities and powers. The mainstream church reacted not by correcting their teaching, but by ignoring the subject completely. To a certain extent this is still true today. The response to error should be truth, not to ignore the subject.

Then as centuries have gone on, again mostly in the West, our focus has been on the individual at the expense of the corporate. When it comes to spiritual warfare, we have begun to talk about it but only in the context of the battle the individual has with Satan and his demons. We have largely ignored the work of evil in society, which is what principalities and powers are about. I am convinced that prejudice and racism are spiritual issues, and we need to fight them with spiritual weapons. They are expressed by individuals, but can also be systemic societal and organisational issues.

A few introductory thoughts on principalities and powers

Principalities and powers are shorthand for a variety of terms Paul employed to refer to powers that are created by God

---

27. Marva J. Dawn, *Powers, Weakness, and the Tabernacling of God* (Schaff Lectures/ Pittsburgh Theological Seminary) (Grand Rapids, MI: Eerdmans: 2001), Kindle location 6.

but have been corrupted and become in some way hostile to Christ and his church and the purposes of God. Paul is speaking of a spiritual dimension of the created order. These are not the same as the devil and demons but part of his evil empire.

Can I remind you of just a few of the key New Testament scriptures that speak of principalities and powers?

> That power is the same as the mighty strength he exerted when he raised Christ from the dead and seated him at his right hand in the heavenly realms, far above all rule and authority, power and dominion, and every name that is invoked, not only in the present age but also in the one to come. And God placed all things under his feet and appointed him to be head over everything for the church, which is his body, the fullness of him who fills everything in every way.
> *(Ephesians 1:19-23)*

> Finally, be strong in the Lord and in his mighty power. Put on the full armour of God, so that you can take your stand against the devil's schemes. For our struggle is not against flesh and blood, but against the rulers, against the authorities, against the powers of this dark world and against the spiritual forces of evil in the heavenly realms.
> *(Ephesians 6:10-12)*

> The Son is the image of the invisible God, the firstborn over all creation. For in him all things were created: things in heaven and on earth, visible and invisible,

whether thrones or powers or rulers or authorities; all things have been created through him and for him.

(Colossians 1:15-16)

There is obviously a lot that could be said from these verses, but there are a few points I want to specifically mention.

Firstly, these powers and authorities were created by Christ but are now against him and his purposes. They are evil spiritual forces.

They are under the authority of Christ and therefore defeated. This means that as Christians we have authority over them. We are not talking about forces with the same power as Christ, not equal and opposite forces. Paul only talks about them in relationship to the superior power we have over them in Christ; however powerful principalities and powers are, the power we have in Jesus is greater.

They are presented as being different from Satan, different from fallen angels and demons. They use human structures, traditions and institutions, they are at work in them, but they are separate from them. Social, political, judicial and economic structures can become influenced by the demonic and become evil, but they are not inevitably so. Every good gift of God can be perverted for evil use. These powers are at work in the world around us; evil doesn't just attack people, it attacks society. Our battle isn't 'against flesh and blood', says Paul.

I find that recognising that there are evil forces at work in society helps me understand the world I live in. For example, mob and gang behaviours which are more than the sum of their parts. It helps me understand societies that go evil, atrocities such as genocide and the breakdown in justice that can happen in some societies. Such things are difficult to understand if it is just the influence of sinful individuals; I think it is much more than that. It explains workplaces that become toxic where bullying and lying are endemic and no one feels able to speak out.

An understanding of principalities and powers and spiritual warfare helps us understand the constant flow of stories of church leaders falling to temptation, either through sexual sin or the misuse of money or power to control others. I think there are forces at work wider than just individuals giving in to temptations. The church is itself a battleground. We are too often unaware of the work of Satan as he seeks to undermine the work of God and the establishing of his kingdom through the demonic and through principalities and powers.

When I consider the world today and in the past, there seem to be forces at work that keep the poor impoverished and create division between rich and poor. This happens within nations and between nations. The complexity of climate change could be an example of this – richer countries creating the problems, running their air conditioning while poorer parts of the world become uninhabitable due to the soaring temperature.

To quote Andy McCullough:

> In the North, eco-theology is a luxury for academics. In the South, it is grass-roots basic Christianity. Our growing interconnectedness as a global body of Christ should alert us to the fact that environmental devastation is one of the clearest forms of inequality and injustice there is. Rich countries appropriate, destroy, profit and grow

richer, while the impact is felt by the poorest among our brothers and sisters. Those most affected are the least responsible, and those most responsible are the least affected. Climate change is racist... 'God so loved the world' certainly does not exclusively mean 'God so loved humans'.[28]

When our eyes are open to it, there are spiritual forces at work everywhere we look. I can find no other viable explanation for what I see – principalities and powers working through human institutions, keeping the world divided through injustice such as poverty, religion, political views, colour and ethnicity.

It is in these terms that we can understand institutional racism as an example of the principalities and powers that Paul talks about. Institutional racism is an example of principalities and powers in operation in institutions. This can even include the church. Understanding principalities and powers will help us understand what we are up against and how we can combat them.

We need to resist the temptation to say that human institutions are of themselves evil; however, evil forces can and do use them. That is what we mean by principalities and powers. Therefore, it is not that the institution itself is racist, but that forces of racism are working within institutions. It is also worth acknowledging that if principalities and powers operate in institutions, the most obvious target is the church, which is where the most damage can be done.

---

28. McCullough, *Made Flesh*, pp. 82-84.

What are they like?

These forces arrayed against us have three main characteristics.

Firstly, they are powerful

Whether 'principalities' and 'powers' refer to different ranks of evil spirits in the hierarchy of hell we do not know, but all the titles given to them draw attention to the power and authority they wield. They are also called the world rulers of 'this present darkness' (Ephesians 6:12, ESV). We have the devil's claim to be able to give Jesus 'all the kingdoms of the world' (Matthew 4:8). Jesus gave the devil the title 'the ruler of this world' (John 14:30, ESV), and 1 John 5:19 tells us that 'the whole world is under the control of the evil one'.

These texts do not deny our Lord's decisive conquest of the principalities and powers, but indicate that as usurpers they have not conceded defeat or been destroyed. So, they continue to exercise considerable power as part of Satan's evil empire.

There is a well-known example of the end of the Second World War. When the Allies established a bridgehead in Normandy, the result of the war was certain, but fighting continued for months with many more casualties until the final Nazi surrender. These evil forces are defeated but are still very powerful; there is still a battle. I believe we experience the battle head-on when it comes to prejudice and its impact in the world.

Secondly, they are wicked

Power itself is neutral; it can be well used or misused. But our spiritual enemies use their power destructively rather than constructively, for evil not for good. They are the worldwide rulers of this present darkness. They hate the light and shrink from it. Darkness is their natural habitat, the darkness of falsehood and sin. They are also described as the 'spiritual hosts of wickedness' (Ephesians 6:12, ASV), which operate in the heavenly places, that is, in the sphere of invisible reality.

They are 'spiritual agents from the very headquarters of evil' (Ephesians 6:13, Phillips). So 'darkness 'and 'wickedness' characterise their actions.

The appearance of Christ on earth was the signal for an unprecedented outburst of activity on the part of the realm of darkness controlled by these world rulers. Extreme wickedness confronted Jesus: he overcame them all.

If we hope to overcome them, we shall need to bear in mind that they have no moral principles, no code of honour, no higher feelings. They recognise no Geneva Convention to restrict or partially civilise the weapons of their warfare. They are utterly unscrupulous, and ruthless in the pursuit of their malicious designs.

Racism and prejudice are evil and shy away from the light; hence it is not always easy to recognise their presence.

Thirdly, they are cunning

Paul writes of the wiles of the devil, and that we are not 'unaware of his schemes' (2 Corinthians 2:11). It is because the devil seldom attacks openly, preferring darkness to light, that when he transforms himself into 'an angel of light' (2 Corinthians 11:14) we are caught unsuspecting.

He is a dangerous wolf but enters Christ's flock in the disguise of a sheep. Sometimes he roars like a lion, but more often is as subtle as a serpent.

The wiles of the devil take many forms, but he is at his wiliest when he succeeds in persuading people that he does not exist. Or to limit his sphere of operation. To deny his reality is to expose ourselves to his subtlety.

Even if we acknowledge the devil, too often we limit his sphere of operation to impacting individuals. We ignore his wider work in society through principalities and powers, especially when it comes to racism and prejudice.

We face opposition that is powerful, wicked and cunning. We need to be aware, alert.

Prejudice and racism as a spiritual issue

Principalities and powers are in the business of building walls, in using differences to create division. This can be between different ethnicities and cultures. Spiritual forces are at work that we need to resist.

John Stott's commentary on Ephesians is called *God's New Society*. He sees the purpose of the letter to the Ephesians is to outline what that new society looks like. He therefore sees Paul's discussion on principalities and powers in this context:

> Is God's plan to create a new society? Then they will do their utmost to destroy it. Has God through Jesus Christ broken down the walls dividing human beings of different

races and cultures from one another? Then the devil through his agents will strive to rebuild them ... It is with these powers that we are told to wage war, or – to be more precise – to 'struggle'. Paul is wanting to emphasize the reality of our engagement with the powers of evil, and the grim necessity of hand-to-hand combat.[29]

It is interesting to note the areas that Stott focuses on as the work of evil in society. He was writing nearly fifty years ago, when breaking down the walls that divided races and cultures was spoken about far less than today. I can remember reading the commentary decades ago and not noticing this comment and other similar references.

We need to do battle, fight for the society, the world, that God desires. Recognising that it is a spiritual battle!

How do we resist these powers?

At a very basic level we need to be aware of them, identify them and declare and demonstrate Christ's victory over them. This is true when it comes to prejudice and racism that we see in operation in society as a whole and where it occurs within the church.

We then need to do battle; Paul gives us detailed instructions of how we do that in Ephesians 6:10-20:

> Finally, be strong in the Lord and in his mighty power. Put on the full armour of God, so that you can take your

---

29. John Stott, *The Message of Ephesians: God's New Society* (London: IVP, 1979), Kindle edition, p. 259.

stand against the devil's schemes. For our struggle is not against flesh and blood, but against the rulers, against the authorities, against the powers of this dark world and against the spiritual forces of evil in the heavenly realms. Therefore put on the full armour of God, so that when the day of evil comes, you may be able to stand your ground, and after you have done everything, to stand. Stand firm then, with the belt of truth buckled around your waist, with the breastplate of righteousness in place, and with your feet fitted with the readiness that comes from the gospel of peace. In addition to all this, take up the shield of faith, with which you can extinguish all the flaming arrows of the evil one. Take the helmet of salvation and the sword of the Spirit, which is the word of God. And pray in the Spirit on all occasions with all kinds of prayers and requests. With this in mind, be alert and always keep on praying for all the Lord's people. Pray also for me, that whenever I speak, words may be given me so that I will fearlessly make known the mystery of the gospel, for which I am an ambassador in chains. Pray that I may declare it fearlessly, as I should.

We need to be strong in the Lord; we can't do battle on our own, we need help from God, his strength and his armour. We need to be part of his army, the church. It is not God's battle alone, we together have a role to play in the fight; working with him, we have something to contribute to the battle.

I had been taught and even taught others that the armour described by Paul is predominantly defensive. As I have read and reflected more recently, I realise that is misleading. We are meant to be fighting against these spiritual forces, going on the offensive, defeating them. It requires us to engage in a battle, but in the right way, in a Christlike way, non-violently! But not to be passive; we are to take the fight to the enemy.

So, let's look at the armour. I will be giving some pieces more attention than others as is relevant to this discussion.

Belt of truth

Ephesians 6 lists truth first because its absence affects everything. If the belt is in place, it keeps everything together. The belt of truth feels especially relevant in the post-truth age, the age of the lie that we are living in.

What Paul is referring to is firstly the truth of the gospel, which Paul summarises as Christ crucified and raised to life. If we lose sight of the cross, we are lost. We end up with a distortion and are unable to battle the powers of this world. The cross stops us focusing on ourselves, our own comfort and putting feeling good as a priority. Fighting prejudice doesn't always result in us feeling good! As we have seen in previous chapters, the work of reconciliation is at the heart of the gospel, the outworking of the truth we hold.

However, it also means living truly, our lives and our words reflecting truth rather than political manoeuvrings. The belt of truth stops us engaging in the way of the world, its propaganda, manipulations and accusations. It means 'speaking the truth in love' (Ephesians 4:15). Starting in the church but also when we engage in the world.

Exaggerations, even lies, that come so easily to us need to be confronted. Truth is foundational to spiritual warfare. Without it we are lost before we even start. Gossip, half-truths, manipulation are rife in society. They can undermine God's work. We need to confront them with truth. Speaking it in love. We need to call out lies, not allow untruth to stand. Not just in those we disagree with, but call out exaggeration and untruths within our own tribe. This is true generally, but even more so in bringing people from different ethnicities together; there is so much misinformation and accusations that fly around that exaggerate divisions. We need great courage and wisdom in discerning truth and calling out lies. Not believing everything we hear.

A current example of this would be for my Muslim friends to call out the acts of Hamas and other Islamic terrorist organisations as just plain wrong, against all Islamic teaching. In the same spirit, I believe the church needs to call out the mass destruction of Gaza and the killing of innocent civilians.

We need to also make sure we are people of truth and call out the wrongs that are done in the name of Christ and his church. To be very careful in what we believe from social media, not repeating lies even if they support our cause; ultimately, they undermine our truth.

Similarly, as churches, let us be careful not to make massive exaggerations that make us look good. They will surely backfire.

Let us wear the belt of truth, not just to defend ourselves but to enable us to attack injustice.

The breastplate of righteousness or justice

The breastplate is only relevant if we are advancing; it protects life-sustaining organs and is irrelevant if we are running away! The breastplate is obviously the righteousness of Christ, which protects us. We can miss it in our English language translations, but in the original Greek the same word is used for righteousness and justice. Christ's righteousness also conveys a sense of Christ's justice.

I therefore think there is a sense here that we are called to work for justice because our God is a God of justice. Justice is so important when dealing with ethnic and class issues. So often minorities are denied justice in our society, even within our churches.

Like speaking the truth, speaking and working for justice is dangerous in our society. It is spiritual warfare. Hence the need for protection as we step out against the powers at work in our society, even in the church, that seek to oppress. We need protection as we speak up for the victim, the powerless, as we come against the powers of this present darkness.

Shoes of readiness to proclaim the gospel of peace

I find it interesting that Paul speaks about a 'readiness' to proclaim the gospel of peace, rather than proclaim the gospel of peace.

In biblical times, usually only soldiers would wear shoes, which were necessary to protect their feet in battle. Heralds, on the other hand, the people who ran with the good news of victory, wouldn't bother with heavy shoes which would stop them running swiftly for purposes of proclamation.

As valuable as is firm footwear, 'readiness' communicates the holy impatience to get the good news of peace out.

We have this tension: we need to get the word out, we need to proclaim truth, but we need protection.

The shield of faith

Again, the shield of faith is an offensive weapon.

The Roman army's interlocking shields made its attacking thrust virtually invincible. The shields were placed in front of the soldier next to you and then as you moved against the castle or whatever, as fiery arrows rained down, they had little effect. The shield therefore speaks of our need of each other as we battle the powers of the world.

We need to learn such dependence on each other. We need to learn that our communities can become closely knit shields of mutual support to enable us to stand against the fiery darts of the powers that attack us.

I think this is especially important for our children who are in the front line of the battle. We need to be protecting them as they advance with us. We need to be in community to protect our children.

The fiery darts come in different forms – accusations, thoughts of doubt, disobedience, rebellion, lust, malice, fear. We are advancing the kingdom and suddenly thoughts come – 'flaming arrows'. We need the protection of others when they do. We can't stand by ourselves; we are an army. We advance together as we fight against injustice, prejudice and racism.

The sword of the Spirit, the Word of God

We don't just make pronouncements, declaring scriptures to each other and the world, we live lives formed by the Word of God; the truth of the Bible shaping us so that we create communities that demonstrate by both word and deed what God's kingdom looks like.

Then finally – prayer always

Prayer is foundational. It recognises our need of God, the fact that we can't do things without God. It is powerful when people from different, diverse backgrounds, different church traditions, different cultural experiences, people from across the age ranges come together in prayer. This more than anything makes a statement, takes the battle to the enemy, and declares the truth of the gospel; we are all one in Christ, whatever background we come from.

Let us acknowledge that prayer is not easy, especially with others who are different from us. Yet when we do it, we feel uplifted and energised – certainly I do. However, it requires humility, it requires acknowledging that even how we pray can be culturally conditioned. We all have our own traditions of prayer. I have found it enlightening to learn from others' experience and practice of prayer.

I am sure that praying together with people who are different from us is the most effective way of building the diverse community God intends. It is probably the closest we can get to the age to come until Christ returns.

Questions to ponder

- How does an understanding of principalities and powers help you understand the world around us better?

- In what ways are you aware of principalities and powers being at work in society as a whole and then in your personal circumstances?

- How are you utilising the armour of God as you do battle with the powers of this current age, especially when it comes to racism and injustice?

5.

The Role of Multicultural Church in Evangelism

Having looked at the type of church God wants and some of the challenges we face in building such a church, we return to the impact such a church could make on the world. I keep mentioning the role that multicultural church could play in wider society quoting ninety-year-old civil rights leader John Perkins: 'There is no institution on earth more equipped and capable of bringing transformation to the cause of reconciliation than the church. But we have some hard work to do.'[30]

When the church models something of how God requires things to be, it can play a special role in race relations that others are ill-equipped to play, but I believe the church has abdicated its responsibility.

I believe that a church that seeks to honour both unity and diversity is also best equipped to reach out in evangelism.

---

30. Perkins, *One Blood*, p. 63.

There are different reasons for believing this, both biblical and experiential reasons. This is what we will be looking at in this chapter.

Firstly, biblical reasons quoting Jesus!

John records a lengthy prayer that Jesus offers to his Father in the hours before his death. Among other things he prays:

> My prayer is not for them alone. I pray also for those who will believe in me through their message, that all of them may be one, Father, just as you are in me and I am in you. May they also be in us so that the world may believe that you have sent me.
>
> *(John 17:20-21)*

As has already been mentioned, unity out of diversity mirrors the Trinity, where three become one without losing their individuality. Jesus here describes his relationship with his Father and prays that we may have the same unity as they have. He also prays that we, those who have believed because of the apostles' message, would be united with the Godhead. The reason for praying for our unity out of diversity is given, 'that the world may believe'. An incredible thought. Jesus prays for us, for you and me; can you imagine if writings of Shakespeare were found that mentioned you by name? He prays we 'may be one' as he and his Father are one so that the world might believe. If we needed any further motivation for united, diverse churches, we can't do better than this verse. Jesus is praying for us to be unity in diversity, so that the world might believe.

Bruce Milne says that Jesus' prayer is 'like a mountaineer gazing out from an eminence across the expanding vista as range succeeds range into the distant horizon, so Jesus gazes out across the rolling centuries. He beholds and embraces the harvest of the ages, the church of the Redeemer, gathered from every nation, people, language and tribe. He is praying for us.'[31]

I have known what it is to not believe and then have my eyes opened to see the truth; the truth that there is a Creator who knows and cares for me, who wants a relationship with me, wants my very best and paid a great price that I might have the best. I guess you have too. My experience has motivated me to want others to know what I know, to see what I see. Knowing that our unity plays a part in this is significant.

Jesus prays for a supernatural unity for his church that is tangible and visible. It is a unity that produces faith in those who encounter it. A church where everyone is so bound together in love that those looking in can say, 'Look how these people love each other.' They will see something of the power of God at work. Such unity gives witness to the work of God, it is not humanly possible!

Commentators from different contexts recognise this truth. Kuzuli Kosse says that in Africa unity is usually found through common family ties, common language or living in the same geographical region. In contrast, the unity of the church extends to all believers of all nations, denominations and

---

31. Bruce Milne, *The Message of John* (Leicester: IVP, 1993), p. 247.

times. He says the local church should transcend tribalism, ethnicity and denominationalism to demonstrate to the world the unity of God's people. 'He [Jesus] knew that unity lends credibility to the message of the church and is part of its mission.'[32]

Roland Allen, a high church missionary to China in the early years of the twentieth century, wrote about how Jesus' prayer works out in his context. He saw that the church in China was special because:

> The profound distinctions which separate race from race only minister to the revelation of Christ's universality. If the West finds in Christ its ideal, so does the East. If Christ can attract the Western mind and heart to Himself, so He is seen to attract a mind and heart which is most unlike, most unapproachable by the Western mind. The more we emphasize the gulf, the more we show, not that Christianity is unsuited to the one because it is suited to the other, but that the Christ is the Divine Master who reconciles the irreconcilable.[33]

In all contexts the great diversity of the church demonstrates an attractive alternative to 'cultural relativism'. It stops people from separating out black Christianity from white Christianity.

> The multiethnic church challenges these assessments by presenting the gospel as something that holds for

---

32. Tokunboh Adeyemo, ed., *African Bible Commentary* (Nairobi, WordAlive, 2006), p. 1314.
33. Roland Allen, *Missionary Principles – and Practice* (Cambridge: The Lutterworth Press, 1913, 2006), Kindle location 604.

people everywhere, and which is visibly followed by all ethnicities.[34]

The multicultural church bears witness to the saving power of Christ to redeem and transform fallen men and women into the likeness of Christ whatever background they come from.

How this might work in practice

The work of evangelism is a community act; we are not called to be anglers but fishermen and fisherwomen working together in fishing teams. It is our Western individualism that puts the focus on us as individuals, missing the community role in fishing. Jesus had never seen an angler in his life. When he calls us to be fishers of men, he is expecting us to follow the pattern of the fishing teams that worked the sea of Galilee, where everyone played their part in catching fish.

I first encountered fishing teams on a visit to Freetown, Sierra Leone. Walking along the beach we saw fishermen out at sea with a massive net; no boat but many people holding the edge of the net and pulling it to shore, where it was met by others who helped get it on the beach. Once on the beach, many more people joined in sorting the catch. Everyone in the community seemed to have a role – men, women, young, old, all played a part in catching not just a single fish but a great multitude of fish that would enable a community to be fed for a while. I saw Jesus' prediction,

---

34. www.cambridgepapers.org/unity-and-diversity-the-church-race-and-ethnicity/ (accessed 9.10.24).

'from now on you will fish for people' (Luke 5:10), in a whole new light. Fishing is a community enterprise, to not just catch individuals but to impact and reach communities for Christ. Surely that is what we should be longing and working for. That is what we do together, people from different cultures and backgrounds, rather than just as individuals.

Additionally, the health and wealth of the community depended on the catch. If there were no fish caught, no one ate. That was true both by the sea of Galilee and in Freetown. Therefore, planning and strategy went into catching fish. Jesus was saying the same planning that previously had gone into catching fish, the same intensity and focus, was now to be present when catching men and women for Christ.

Putting Luke 5:10 alongside John 17:21, we see that part of our intentional focus on winning men and women for Christ should be in diverse fishing teams, the church, demonstrating something of the power of the gospel that breaks down all barriers and is available for all.

The preacher may declare the message, but we cannot leave it just to the preacher; their message is backed up and demonstrated by a fellowship of believers in supernatural love with one another across all natural boundaries. The multicultural church that loves across all barriers and differences is exactly what Jesus prays for; it is a visible display of the fruits of the gospel message. It enables the world to believe.

This idea of working in teams relates across churches as well as within local churches. I have found this to be essential in the context of Luton. To create a context where both our Muslim and secular neighbours listen to us, we must all work together across denominational boundaries and across racial boundaries. Not in competition with other churches, but as part of a cross-town fishing team. I am aware that we have more in common with other churches serving the same community than those of the same denomination serving very different contexts. It requires us to break out of the privatised religion secularists prefer! My experience is that it causes unchurched people to notice us in a way they do not for individual congregations.

In Luton we have a few multicultural churches but also many monocultural churches that are Asian, African and Caribbean as well as white British. I have found that I can learn so much from these churches and from their leaders. Occasionally, I have even found them learning from me! This process of learning from churches from different ethnic backgrounds and working together with them has been particularly important following the death of George Floyd and the resultant grappling with racism in society as a whole and within the church.

We have been able to create contexts where ethnic leaders can share their experience of racism not just in the world but also within the church. White church leaders have been able to respond, sharing their own complicity and asking for and receiving forgiveness. We have eaten meals together, prayed together, declared our determination to do all we can to eliminate racism. This has been noted by the town as a whole, and our work as church leaders has been seen as an example for others to follow. A personal highlight for me was preaching at a black majority church and confessing my own racism and asking for forgiveness, which was lovingly offered. I am told by their pastor that many stereotypes of white church leaders were broken that Sunday.

Malawian academic Harvey Kwiyani, based in the UK, says:

> I am also convinced that the multicultural context of (urban) Britain needs a multicultural missionary movement. African, Latin American, Asian and British Christians need to work together in mission. For that to happen, there needs to be some intentional collaboration. Congregational leaders may need to model this for their followers by working together more visibly. I anticipate that the body of Christ in Britain can model racial reconciliation for the world by living an alternative reality where all races are one in Christ. Such a church may be a critical missional testimony to the world that the love of Christ can set people free.[35]

This is true at a local level, such as where I am in Luton, as well as at a national level.

Other practical examples of us working together as churches include a regular publication highlighting how churches and Christian organisations are serving the town, and town-wide outreach events, sometimes organised centrally by Churches Together in Luton, at other times organised by a local church and supported by other churches.

The best example is the cooperation between churches in serving refugees: one church focuses on practical needs, which include a regular drop-in with clothes distribution and advocacy work; another church offers free English language

---

35. Kwiyani, *Multicultural Kingdom*, p. 93.

lessons. Between the churches there are numerous Bible studies using different resources that complement each other. We are together presenting the gospel to our neighbours. The result is many refugees coming to faith. I know this is dismissed in some circles as fraudulent, that refugees are claiming faith to aid their right-to-remain application. By working together as churches, we can put together long-term discipleship programmes that seek to reduce the potential of this happening. We are also mutually accountable in ensuring that, as far as we are able, professed conversions are authentic.

Another initiative being explored in Luton is 'Christians Together for an estate'. Gathering all Christians from whatever church who live in a certain area of the town, usually an estate, to get to know each other and identify how together they might serve the area. This activity is supported by all the churches in the town and enables believers from diverse ethnicities and denominations to build relationships and serve their area, while staying active worshipping members of their church. In doing so, they present a united witness to their community and are able together to address the unique needs of their neighbours, whether that is knife crime or loneliness.

There are other experiential reasons that the multicultural church has an important role to play in the UK today

I came across this quote in *The Times* newspaper on 1 October 2012:

> Christianity has now become a foreign language for very large numbers of the population and what goes on in church seems strange, if not alien. Until about 1960, what went on in church would have some resonance across the culture as a whole. We now have the third and fourth generation growing up since then for whom it is simply outside their world view. Failures that tend to be blamed on schools or parents simply reflect a rapid and massive change in the general culture.[36]

I paraphrase this as 'for the vast majority of people in the UK today the church is an alien culture, and Christianity is a foreign language'. If we are unable to engage with fellow Christians from different languages and cultures, how are we going to engage with those who are not believers, who live with a different worldview from us? If we are to reach people outside the church, we need to be able to relate and communicate with people who are different from us. Where better to start than with those who are also part of the body of believers but who are different from us? Additionally, even if we reach people with the gospel, we need to create communities into which they can be welcomed and flourish.

The parable of the sower in Matthew 13 informs us that many who respond to the word do not persevere; however, the parable encourages us to do all we can to ensure as great a harvest as possible. We are meant to ensure as much seed as possible falls on good ground. Communities that value and

---

36. *The Times* (London), 1 October 2012. Original not found.

accommodate people from many different backgrounds are an important part of this.

All that we have seen previously of the reasons we struggle to relate to people who are different from us, fear of what people think, fear of getting things wrong, feelings of inferiority or superiority, all apply to how we feel about those who are outside the church. We need to overcome these barriers with unbelievers as well as with fellow believers.

Harvey Kwiyani suggests that 'a community that builds walls to keep strangers out only imprisons itself within its own walls in the end. A prison guard is also a prisoner'.[37]

A failure to engage with people who are different from us will ultimately result in the decline of any local church. We must move out of our comfort zones relationally, the very future of the church is at stake, as Jesus warned us.

Our nation needs to be re-evangelised. New generations need to hear the gospel for the first time. We must earn the right to be heard; people are not flocking to hear our sermons, preaching in the open-air doesn't draw crowds, let alone conversions. I believe we together demonstrate the gospel though communities of faith that are breaking down barriers, communities that seek to serve the wider community we are part of – we then find that we earn the right to give a 'reason for the hope' (1 Peter 3:15) within us that motivates us to do these things.

I am convinced that God is calling us to have the courage needed to build such communities.

---

37. Kwiyani, *Multicultural Kingdom*, p. 95.

Questions to ponder

- In what ways do building healthy relationships with people who are different from us help us be more effective in evangelism?
- What are you motivated to change, having read the chapter?
- How can you help churches in your context work together across denominational and ethnic boundaries? What are the barriers to this happening?

6.

The Importance of Humility

In previous chapters we have looked at why we should be seeking to build multicultural churches, the benefits of doing so and some of the challenges. Over the next few chapters, we start to look at some of the key elements of how to build such churches, starting with the need for humility.

Over recent years, I have become increasingly convinced of the central importance of humility for the Christian. It is at the heart of being a follower of Christ. We are called to humble ourselves before the Lord for him to lift us up (James 4:10). To become a Christian requires us to acknowledge our total dependence on him, to realise that we cannot save ourselves but must rely fully on the grace of God. I am also increasingly aware that humility is central as we outwork the gospel both as individuals and as churches. Humility is not only key to enter the kingdom, it is key to living out kingdom values. Humility is essential if we want to build multicultural churches, churches that value people who are different from us. To do so we need humility; it is impossible without it. Hopefully, if you have got this far, you are motivated to be involved in building with people who are different from yourself. In which case an initial step is to seek to grow in humility.

Too often, instead of humility it is easy to slip into an attitude of pride – pride in our background, pride in our culture, pride in our denomination, pride in our church. Pride gets in the way; humility enables us to build with people and churches who are different from us. James and Peter both tell us that 'God opposes the proud but shows favour to the humble' (James 4:6; 1 Peter 5:5).

Humility is therefore an essential place to start as we look at the foundations required to build churches that value and honour people from very different backgrounds and life experiences.

Ethiopian theologian Eshetu Abate says, 'Unity is a mark of strength. An Amharic proverb from Ethiopia says, "Threads united can tie even a lion." Paul's call to unity applies to divided Christendom, and to every local church in which division and party strife are spoiling fellowship and marring the witness.' He continues with the factors that cause disunity that include vanity, a lack of humility, looking down on others, and focusing on one's own interests.[38]

My experience is that not only is humility an essential foundation for multicultural churches, but also multicultural churches facilitate growth in humility.

We will be spending this chapter looking at humility through two scriptures: one from Mark's Gospel, the other from Paul's letter to the church in Philippi.

---

38. Adeyemo, ed., *African Bible Commentary*, p. 1468.

Humility in Mark 9 and 10

A major strand of Jesus' teaching is what true greatness looks like, defined by the sort of person we should strive to become as his followers. Jesus' definition of greatness was at odds with the consensus of both his day and ours. Jesus says that the truly great person is someone who serves, a servant. To serve you must be humble; proud people don't serve. In the world, great people have servants, people who do their bidding. Jesus is saying to be great you need to do the Father's bidding, to give up your status, rank and power. This is demonstrated by Jesus when he shocked the disciples by washing their feet (John 13).

Before we go into detail, it is worth noting that there is a big but subtle difference between someone who really wants to be great in the eyes of others – therefore hearing this teaching they will seek to serve to look good – and the person who is great because they serve.

The truth demonstrated by Jesus in washing the disciples' feet is also developed very clearly in Mark 9 and 10.

Jesus predicts his death a second time: Mark 9

Jesus and his disciples are purposefully on their final journey towards Jerusalem where he was going to die. A series of events happened on the way that are recorded by Mark. Two are particularly significant, one from chapter 9 and another from chapter 10.

> They left that place and passed through Galilee. Jesus did not want anyone to know where they were, because

he was teaching his disciples. He said to them, 'The Son of Man is going to be delivered into the hands of men. They will kill him, and after three days he will rise.' But they did not understand what he meant and were afraid to ask him about it.

They came to Capernaum. When he was in the house, he asked them, 'What were you arguing about on the road?' But they kept quiet because on the way they had argued about who was the greatest.

Sitting down, Jesus called the Twelve and said, 'Anyone who wants to be first must be the very last, and the servant of all.'

(Mark 9:30-35)

There is a very similar incident in the next chapter. The similarity is important, as is the repetition of the central point that is being made. This becomes clear reading them one after the other.

Jesus predicts his death a third time: Mark 10

They were on their way up to Jerusalem, with Jesus leading the way, and the disciples were astonished, while those who followed were afraid. Again he took the Twelve aside and told them what was going to happen to him. 'We are going up to Jerusalem,' he said, 'and the Son of Man will be delivered over to the chief priests and the teachers of the law. They will condemn him to death and will hand him over to the Gentiles, who will mock him and spit on him, flog him and kill him. Three days later he will rise.'

(Mark 10:32-34)

The request of James and John

Then James and John, the sons of Zebedee, came to him. 'Teacher,' they said, 'we want you to do for us whatever we ask.'

'What do you want me to do for you?' he asked.

They replied, 'Let one of us sit at your right and the other at your left in your glory.'

'You don't know what you are asking,' Jesus said. 'Can you drink the cup I drink or be baptised with the baptism I am baptised with?'

'We can,' they answered.

Jesus said to them, 'You will drink the cup I drink and be baptised with the baptism I am baptised with, but to sit at my right or left is not for me to grant. These places belong to those for whom they have been prepared.'

When the ten heard about this, they became indignant with James and John. Jesus called them together and said, 'You know that those who are regarded as rulers of the Gentiles lord it over them, and their high officials exercise authority over them. Not so with you. Instead, whoever wants to become great among you must be your servant, and whoever wants to be first must be slave of all. For even the Son of Man did not come to be served, but to serve, and to give his life as a ransom for many.

(Mark 10:35-45)

In both incidents we clearly see the contrast between Jesus and his disciples. The humility of Jesus as he predicts his death, which is the extreme and ultimate example of his humility and of serving others. This is immediately followed by shocking examples of the disciples' pride and arrogance. Jesus lovingly corrects them, seeking to help them see a new way of living and thinking. We are meant to see ourselves in the disciples, but to then desire to become more like Jesus.

For the disciples, greatness was linked to selfish ambition; they wanted positions of power, and were even willing to use Jesus to achieve it. It is so easy for us to want greatness at the expense of any or everyone. We can even seek to use Jesus for our own ends! The disciples are men receiving intensive training from Jesus, yet they knew no better. It is so easy to compare ourselves to others and look for opportunities to claim greater importance than them. Human nature is such that we don't really want to be rich, just richer than others; we don't want power, we want more power than others. We want to be great, which really means greater than others. This is the attitude that goes on to see our culture, our clan, our people as better than others. This is the way of the world all around us; we elevate ourselves and our people above others. In this way we can even create unity and a sense of belonging, a sense of team by emphasising and contrasting ourselves to those who are different from us – we are better than them. We create an antipathy to people outside our group. We are united, we are proud to be better than them.

All this is the opposite to the way of Christ, the way of the cross.

Significantly, Jesus does not categorically criticise or forbid the desire and ambition to be great. Instead, he clearly redirects that ambition, redefines it and purifies it:

> But whoever would be great among you must be your servant, and whoever would be first among you must be slave of all.
>
> *(Mark 10:43b-44, ESV)*

> If anyone would be first, he must be last of all and servant of all.
>
> *(Mark 9:35, ESV)*

Serving others for the glory of God, this is the genuine expression of humility; this is true greatness as the Saviour defined it.

This is so important for us as individuals and as churches. A great church is therefore a serving church. A great person is therefore one who serves. We are meant to see and apply the contrast between Jesus and the way of the world; the way of the world is driven by our natural inclinations.

Jesus is a model for us, in contrast to the disciples and the world. He is also our Saviour. We cannot free ourselves from pride and selfish ambition; a divine rescue is necessary. It is not a coincidence that these episodes are in the context of Jesus talking about his death.

> For even the Son of Man did not come to be served, but to serve, and to give his life as a ransom for many.
>
> *(Mark 10:45)*

James and John were ransomed by the Saviour's death and forgiven of their pride and all their sins. And they would be transformed as well, from self-confident men into humble servants who would live to serve others with the gospel for the glory of God. And they would suffer.

And the explanation for this transformation wasn't just our Lord's example but our Lord's sacrifice, his life for ours. The cross ransoms, the cross liberates, the cross transforms! We can't feign humility; we can't be proud of our humility; it's Jesus' death that enables us to follow his example.

True humility, our own service to others, is always both an effect of his unique sacrifice and the evidence of it.

As Andrew Murray put it so well, 'It is easy to think we humble ourselves before God: humility towards men will be the only sufficient proof that our humility before God is real.'[39]

Humility is at the heart of the gospel; it is the fruit and evidence of the sacrifice of Christ. Humility shows itself in our relationship with others.

These very same truths are taught by Paul in Philippians 2:1-11

Philippians is unusual among the letters of Paul in that it was not written in response to problems in the church that he was aware of, but in response to a gift that he had received. It is therefore helpful in identifying what Paul emphasises when he doesn't have to address problems in the church. He starts by reassuring them that they shouldn't worry because

---

39. www.biblestudytools.com/classics/murray-humility/humility-in-daily-life (accessed 28.10.24).

he is in prison, that will not affect the spread of the gospel. He then exhorts them to conduct themselves 'in a manner worthy of the gospel of Christ' (1:27). The root of the word translated 'worthy' implies 'in balance'. We live worthy lives when our lives are in balance with our beliefs. What a worthy life, a life in balance, looks like is spelt out at the beginning of chapter 2. Worthy lives are lives of humility, as humility is at the heart of the gospel, the heart of what we believe.

Imitating Christ's humility: Philippians 2

> Therefore if you have any encouragement from being united with Christ, if any comfort from his love, if any common sharing in the Spirit, if any tenderness and compassion, then make my joy complete by being like-minded, having the same love, being one in spirit and of one mind. Do nothing out of selfish ambition or vain conceit. Rather, in humility value others above yourselves, not looking to your own interests but each of you to the interests of the others.
>
> In your relationships with one another, have the same mindset as Christ Jesus:
>
> who, being in very nature God,
>   did not consider equality with God something to be
>   used to his own advantage;
> rather, he made himself nothing
>   by taking the very nature of a servant,
>   being made in human likeness.

And being found in appearance as a man,
   he humbled himself
   by becoming obedient to death –
      even death on a cross!

Therefore God exalted him to the highest place
   and gave him the name that is above every name,
that at the name of Jesus every knee should bow,
   in heaven and on earth and under the earth,
and every tongue acknowledge that Jesus
   Christ is Lord,
   to the glory of God the Father.

(Philippians 2:1-11)

Christ's very incarnation was an expression of humility. He did not cling to his divine rights but emptied himself by becoming a man. This does not mean that Christ in any way ceased to be God. The depth of the humility shown is amazing. Jesus could have beamed down as a grown man, but he chose to be born as a baby. He could at least have been born in a palace, but chose a manger where animals fed. He could have been born into a rich or influential family but instead was born into poverty and became a carpenter. He could have been born in an important city like Rome or Jerusalem but chose rural Bethlehem.

Jesus not only chose to empty himself, but he also never told anybody he had done this. Neither did Jesus have a need to get anybody's approval. Can you imagine Jesus saying to the disciples after the Sermon on the Mount, 'How did I do? I think that went well. What do you think,

Peter?' Jesus got his approval from the Father. He 'emptied himself' (Philippians 2:7, ASV) and didn't feel he needed to prove himself to anyone.

Again, what an example we see in Jesus and what a contrast to the way of the world.

The gospel is the source of all true humility; it is knowing the good news that we have been accepted by the Father through faith not by works that enables us to see we do not seek to gain the approval of people. We have the approval of the Creator of the universe. Humility is not a virtue we cultivate in the abstract; it is a mark of integrity to the gospel, and all our efforts at humility must be fuelled by the gospel lest they result in mere fleshly counterfeits or imitations.

If our understanding of greatness is rooted in Christ, we should desire as individuals to be great. We should desire churches to be great. I long for there to be great churches. But we need to make sure our understanding of greatness is right, otherwise we will climb up the ladder only to find it is leaning against the wrong wall. We move towards greatness by serving, by considering others as better than ourselves, continually asking the question, as individuals and churches, who are we serving? Not seeking accolades for doing so other than the 'well done' (Matthew 25:21) from our Father in heaven.

If we are to properly work with those who are different from ourselves, we must have the same attitude as Jesus, valuing others above ourselves.

In some circles people talk about resource churches. I would suggest that perhaps it would be much better to be called serving churches! Resource church can convey the attitude of superiority: 'We are better than you, we have more than you, which we would like to share.' Resource churches can be patronising. Serving churches ask, 'Who can we serve?' They convey something more of the heart of the gospel – humility.

I hope I have made the point of the central place of humility in not just entering the Christian life, but also living the Christian life. Humility is the opposite and antidote to pride, the biggest challenge we face.

R.T. Kendall is helpful:

> I therefore define pride essentially as taking oneself too seriously. Taking oneself too seriously is the common denominator in all proud people. It describes those who resent criticism, who are insecure, who cannot laugh at themselves, whose need of praise is constant, who see themselves as overly important, who fancy themselves as being very special to God (and think God bends the rules for them), who tend to blame others for their problems, who hate taking the blame, who cannot bear not getting the credit for the good they did, and who have an insatiable need to prove themselves.[40]

Such an attitude of pride will stop us relating healthily to people who are different from us. It will stop us seeking to serve them. It will also stop us from seeking to learn from them, even recognising we can learn from them.

To truly be serious and deliberate in mortifying pride and cultivating greatness, we must make a conscious decision to

---

40. R.T. Kendall, *The Power of Humility: Living Like Jesus* (Lake Mary, FL: Charisma House, 2011), Kindle edition, p. 8.

do so. A healthy place to start is to each day remind ourselves of the cross. When we do that, as the hymn says:

> My richest gain I count but loss,
> And pour contempt on all my pride.[41]

'God ... gives grace to the humble' (James 4:6). Contrary to popular and false belief, it's not 'those who help themselves' whom God helps; it's those who humble themselves.[42]

The role of humility in unity and diversity

A barrier to building united churches that value diversity is pride, considering our culture as superior to others. This was the cause of many of the problems that Paul addressed in his letters: Jews feeling themselves superior to Gentile believers and therefore requiring them to become like them; unity but without celebrating diversity. The antidote is to consider others better than ourselves – humility.

This doesn't come naturally. It doesn't come naturally to me, a white educated male. My wife keeps pointing out to me the irony of me wanting to tell everyone of the insights that I have discovered, feeling that I have something to contribute, and the danger of that taking precedence over me learning from others. I know the theory but continually struggle to put it into practice.

---

41. Isaac Watts (1674-1748), https://hymnary.org/text/when_i_survey_the_wondrous_cross_watts (accessed 11.11.24).
42. C.J. Mahaney, *Humility: True Greatness* (New York: Multnomah Publishers, 2005), Kindle edition, p. 19.

Too often we value our Britishness with pride; not to do so seems unpatriotic. This is seen in the way we exported our British way of life at the time of empire, believing we were improving cultures and societies in doing so. We must fight against that mentality today. It shows itself in the way that Brits abroad are expats, but foreigners in the UK are immigrants. It shows itself in some Christian parenting courses that end up teaching that traditional British middle-class parenting is 'biblical' and superior, blind to parenting insights from other cultures and classes. I have seen British families in Spain resist the pattern of kids having a siesta in the afternoon and staying up later in the evening as a point of principle, looking down on the so-called poor parenting of locals. Is it biblical for children to have a set bedtime?

There are so many areas which we need to approach with humility, areas where we can allow our culture to impact practice and beliefs rather than to value insights from other cultures. Other examples include our view of marriage. It is worth asking yourself the question, is love marriage as practised in the West more biblical and superior to the different forms of arranged marriage? We at least should be willing to ask the question with humility, willing to learn from other cultures. Another area to consider is the differing attitudes to older people: how does the State looking after old people rather than their families tie in with Scripture?

Cultures also have different views on the importance of education. For some it is a very high priority, and children are expected to study independently or with a tutor every day after school; children are expected to have very high aspirations. In these cultures, teachers are highly respected and valued. Other cultures have a very different attitude, and

I have heard those who value education highly being accused of making it an idol by people in the church! Everything can be an idol, but we must be so careful in dismissing those whose values are different from ours as being idolators. Jesus clearly said to look at the 'plank' in our own eye before we worry about the 'speck' in others (Matthew 7:1-5). It is not for us to condemn other cultures; much better to consider and value others higher than ourselves and seek to learn from them.

The list is endless: how are household chores allocated? Attitudes to money and debt; to careers and work; giving to charity; the importance of voting. We need to approach cultural practices with humility.

I asked some friends who were new to British culture what they found most difficult to accept in our way of doing things; below are some of their answers. Worth us humbly reviewing our own culture!

- British people do not talk much.
- Hospitality is different – you don't just pop in, you wait until invited. You can't just pop into people's homes, let alone eat with them unannounced.
- There are different standards of hygiene; dogs and cats are allowed in the house; crockery and cutlery. are dried using dirty tea towels.
- Members of churches drink alcohol.
- People shake hands with members of the opposite sex, even hug.
- The word 'family' is used of the church, but it is not the type of family you expect. I was not invited to

the wedding of the minister's son; I would be if I were family!

- The way some girls dress in short skirts and showing cleavage. I was surprised by how much (almost) nudity there was around on the streets and even in the church.
- I found instant coffee difficult!

We all need humility to learn from and serve others; it is not easy, but it is so helpful and enriching when we do.

Getting to know people who are different from us requires humility. It can also help us grow in humility. As Gavin Ortland says: 'One of the most powerful ways to grow in humility is to embrace situations that make you uncomfortable or exhibit your weakness. We all have certain situations in which we feel vulnerable – times when we are not in control or not at our best, or that draw out our weaknesses.'[43]

For some people, speaking to those who are different from us is outside of our comfort zone. We need to go even further and intentionally seek to get to know people who are different from us. When we do so, humility shows itself in seeking to understand and learn from their culture rather than to just tell them about our culture.

Similarly, when people from different backgrounds come to our church, we will seek to learn from them and see how their experience can complement and enrich ours, rather than just tell them how they need to adapt to fit in!

---

43. Gavin Ortlund, *Humility: The Joy of Self-Forgetfulness* (Wheaton, IL: Crossway, 2023), Kindle edition, p. 43.

Displaying humility is also important in building relationships between churches

The default so often is to see our church and church tradition as superior to others. That was the attitude I imbibed early in my Christian life – the idea and attitude that my church was the best in town. Pride in my church and the superiority of our church is the way of the world impinging on the church. That easily becomes the attitude in church planting; we are coming to town to start a new church because the existing churches are not doing a good job. No wonder church planting has a bad press in many places. A great church will consider others better than themselves. A great church plant will seek to serve and complement the work of existing churches.

It is possible for liturgical churches to look down on the chaos of non-liturgical churches. Non-liturgical churches can question what they see as the lack of freedom in liturgical worship. Andrew Wilson has written an excellent book challenging these attitudes; he challenges us all:

> Contemporary churches that have thrown the liturgical baby out with the formalist bathwater and continue to proudly define themselves that way, even though their meetings are equally predictable and the formalist bathwater has long since evaporated. Or their traditionalist counterparts, where nobody is ever surprised, nobody (except the pastor) uses spiritual gifts, and nobody smiles. Far more common, however, are those churches that, through a combination of history, habit, and the avoidance of extremes, risk being stuck in Bible-church no-man's-land. Suspicious

of anything ancient (because it seems like dead routine) and suspicious of anything fresh (because it seems like a cultural fad), they have opted for worship that is somewhere between twenty and fifty years old, safe but anemic, predictable but ethereal. They are blissfully free of either ritual or emotion, and as a result, they lack body and lack soul.[44]

We have so much to learn from each other, we desperately need the input from those who are different from us; that will only happen if we display humility, considering others better than ourselves.

Let us overcome the temptation to criticise other cultures but to learn from them. Let us lay a foundation of humility in our lives and in our churches that we can then build on to create truly great, multicultural churches.

> ## Questions to ponder
> - Why is humility so foundational to our Christian faith?
> - What can you do to cultivate it and put to death pride?
> - In what ways does pride prevent us building relationships and humility help us?

---

44. Andrew Wilson, *Spirit and Sacrament: An Invitation to Eucharismatic Worship* (Grand Rapids, MI: Zondervan, 2018), Kindle edition, pp. 14-15.

7.

Understanding Culture

Having made the claim that God wants us to build diverse churches where ethnic and cultural distinctives are valued, we are starting to look at how we can facilitate that, looking at what foundations need to be put in place for this to happen.

Gathering people from different cultures is a great first step, but that isn't all that God wants for us. It is easy for churches to celebrate their diversity, with flags across the room showing how many nations are represented in their congregation, but then to leave it there. There is further hard work to be done to create unity amid diversity, so that we do not end up with uniformity. To move forward we need to understand a little about culture, and the impact it can have on our churches. That is the purpose of this chapter.

God's intention isn't for us to gather people from across the globe and for everyone to assimilate and become the same. It is so easy for us to assume that our culture is right and for us unthinkingly to impose it on others, not realising that it is inherited from our country rather than from Scripture. Too often we don't give enough thought to the fact that we all have a culture, that our church has a culture too, and to consider how these cultures match with God's intentions.

As we saw in the last chapter, we need to approach this with humility, being willing to listen to the views of others, even if they express their views in a way that is hard to hear. We can be aware of our Christian heritage, Victorian missionaries building churches in Africa and India that were culturally British and totally out of place with the context. Seeing elaborate church buildings amid extreme poverty in Goa, India, was a shock to me. As tourists we were told that each new bishop wanted to build a more elaborate cathedral than his predecessor. Even more of a shock was to see a church building in Sierra Leone built more recently by American missionaries. It was the only brick building in an area surrounded by poverty; it even had air-conditioning. With the missionaries no longer there, the church could not afford to run the air-conditioning, and the locals didn't need it anyway. More importantly, the building was totally out of place where it was – much more suitable for back in the States. As I have said before, it is so easy to see the speck in other people's eyes but miss the plank in our own (Matthew 7:1-5). We must accept that our culture will have weaknesses that others can see but we are blind to.

We are not all motivated to consider and understand other cultures

Laura Liswood[45] uses the analogy of an elephant and a mouse stuck in a room together. The mouse needs to know

---

45. Laura A. Liswood, *The Loudest Duck: Moving Beyond Diversity While Embracing Differences to Achieve Success at Work* (Hoboken, NJ: Wiley, 2010), Kindle edition, p. 31.

everything about the elephant because otherwise it is liable to be crushed. The elephant doesn't need to know anything about the mouse as it is mighty, tall and powerful. So it is with cultures; the dominant culture has no felt need to understand other cultures, while minority cultures feel the need to know everything they can about the dominant culture to survive, let alone flourish.

If we want to have true unity out of diversity, benefiting from all the unique insights different cultures bring, there is a need to understand the way both our own and other cultures view the world. The ideal is for there to be enough 'mice' in the room that they can confidently speak out and influence the general culture without fearing the elephant. This is why there is a tipping point of around 20 per cent of a congregation being not from the majority culture to begin to effect change. Even then it is important for the majority culture, the elephant, to go out of their way to understand other cultures and to encourage mice to speak up!

Changing our cultural perspectives is not easy but very important

Changing how we view the world is not easy, as we have been taught the world is the way it is since we were young, when we are taught sayings to reinforce our worldview. Liswood compares American, Japanese and Chinese sayings.[46] In the USA people say, 'The squeaky wheel gets the grease', which has the opposite connotation of the Japanese who say, 'The

---

46. Liswood, *The Loudest Duck*, p. 50.

nail that sticks out gets hit on the head' and the Chinese, 'The loudest duck gets shot'. People from the USA view the world from the perspective that the person who complains the loudest gets the most attention, while being outspoken is discouraged in other cultures. Their expectation is that those who speak out will get punished rather than rewarded.

It is important to understand these deep-seated cultural viewpoints if we are to create an environment where all are valued and able to contribute. Otherwise, people from a certain culture will continue to dominate.

Those in positions of authority naturally assume they are there because of their gifting, calling and hard work. Others may feel there is a glass ceiling which certain groups feel unable to burst through and can give up trying. There needs to be an open and honest dialogue if we are to move forward in creating churches that truly value diversity, especially diversity in leadership. Keeping the animal imagery, we can invite lots of different animals onto the ark, but must work hard to understand what our unconscious thoughts tell us and lead us to do with the animals once they are on the ark. We must overcome the subtle advantages or disadvantages that diversity brings with it. We need to be very purposeful in this or we will not be able to create a truly diverse leadership within our churches.

There are so many poor examples of handling diversity in teams; it is so easy to fall into a practice that is 'colonising' and full of tokenism. We really do need to work very hard on this – change takes understanding and then effort.

There is a lot of literature on the characteristics of different cultures, mostly from the secular field, written for international companies to help them get the most out of their employees. There are things we can learn from the world. One of the most important is that leading a diverse organisation requires different leadership skills, which can be learned. Understanding culture is part of this.

Culture can be defined as 'how we do things around here'. Families have their own culture. For example, my family always ate together at a table rather than in front of the TV. When I married, we established this tradition in our own family. Both my boys have established the same pattern with their families.

Whether we realise it or not, churches also have their own culture – for example, the style of music and dress code. I remember inviting a mentor from early in my Christian walk to preach at a church I led. The first thing he did when he arrived was to take off his tie and suit jacket; he realised that our dress code culture was less formal than he had been used to in his own church. A small example but when you feel out of step with the prevailing culture, it can feel deeply uncomfortable.

Experiencing a different culture

Nations also have their own cultures, but of course there are lots of variations within them. There are advantages and disadvantages in generalisations; the advantages are such that it is worth looking at them. People living in a new country can experience culture shock because of the change in culture. Often companies sending people to work abroad prepare them for the culture shock they will experience; good mission organisations do the same. However, many of the people from other cultures arriving at our church may not be aware that such a thing exists; similarly, others in the congregation may not be aware of what is going on. This, in my experience, is true for refugees but also those who have arrived in other ways. So many of the presenting pastoral issues from those newly arrived in the church is due to culture shock.

Dotha Blackwood describes her initial experience of arriving in the UK: 'So the surprise when I came to England was to discover that I was black. I also discovered I was female.'[47]

This has been the experience of many people from across the world, whether they experience racism or not, just the fact that they are different is a shock.

It is worth having a basic understanding of the stages of culture shock and making others aware of them. There is much more information online. Here is a summary.

Stages in culture shock

Honeymoon

When someone first arrives, they have the excitement of a tourist. Everything is new and enjoyable. I love being a tourist, experiencing new cultures, experimenting with different experiences. Many of us enjoy travel because of this. However, our identity is still back home. We enjoy being away, but also love returning.

---

47. Israel Olofinjana, ed., *Turning the Tables on Mission: Stories of Christians from the Global South in the UK* (Watford: Instant Apostle, 2013), Kindle location 3160.

Disorientation

After a while the excitement of the newness is replaced by a sense of being overwhelmed, and a feeling of inadequacy. This was the experience of many I worked with who moved to Spain to plant an international church. When they first arrived, they loved the new context, especially the weather and food. This soon was replaced by frustration. Someone brushed against a poisonous caterpillar and had a very serious and life-threatening rash. Who knew they existed? Handling the bureaucracy involved in making cars legal was overwhelming, especially with little Spanish.

Others coming to the UK experience their own sense of disorientation. When we move within our own nation, we must deal with things like registering with a new doctor and getting dental care. We can find that difficult, but for those who don't understand the system it can be overwhelming. Children settling into new schools with a different syllabus than they are used to is a challenge; it can be overwhelming and can lead to levels of melancholy and despair. They need help and reassurance that what they are feeling is to be expected.

They can also feel uncomfortable in the church, which may be very different from what they are used to. Suddenly they are a minority when they are used to being the majority. The worship may be very different. They will not know the unwritten rules of how to do things. No wonder many people coming to a new context choose to worship with others from their own culture, whether that is British people in Spain or Nigerians in the UK. They need help if they are to settle in a new context.

Irritability and hostility

Disorientation transforms into irritability and hostility, blaming the new culture for their difficulties. My son and his wife lived for several years in India; I remember visiting them when they were going through this stage of culture shock. Their honeymoon period was long gone, and they were very, very irritable. Seeing their hostility to locals was difficult, especially as I was still enjoying the honeymoon stage! Nothing was being done well enough, no local could be trusted, they were all incompetent.

I find it hard when new arrivals to the UK are going through this stage. The natural inclination is to stick up for your country, even if you feel things could improve. We don't like outsiders complaining about us. We can respond either consciously or subconsciously in very unhelpful ways; for example, we can complain about British weather, but we resent it when those coming to our country do – surely they knew about the weather before they arrived! To be told that British schools and teaching methods are worse than those back home in what we consider to be a less affluent country can be grating. The church can be criticised: we may not be preaching the right things, the worship may be flat, the children may not be learning and growing in God as expected. How we react to those suffering culture shock can make things worse. Conflict can result. Knowing such feelings are generally inevitable can help all concerned. The alternative is that many people give up at this stage and return home.

Adjustment and integration

Things do generally get better if people are willing to stick with it. There is an increased ability to function and understand the good and bad in both cultures. Destructive dissatisfaction can become constructive dissatisfaction, and the new people can be a great blessing in helping the church grow and develop, if we are willing to listen and allow it. It can be a relief to all involved when this stage is reached, and leads to great kingdom progress.

Biculturality

Eventually there is the possibility of being fluent and comfortable in both cultures. You can feel at home in both places. In fact, you can be so comfortable in the new culture that you experience reverse culture shock when you return home!

Such people are a great blessing. When we first received many Iranian refugees wanting to be part of the church and to either understand more about Christianity or to grow in their faith, I turned to an Iranian friend from a nearby town who had been in the UK for many years and had reached the stage of being bicultural. He would regularly join us and lead the Bible studies with our Iranians. He could support them, and build appropriate bridges that others couldn't.

A humorous way to see why people coming to the UK can experience culture shock is to look at the nuances in the way we communicate![48]

---

48. Source unknown.

What the British say	What the British mean	What others understand
I hear what you say	I disagree and do not want to discuss it further	He accepts my point of view
With the greatest respect	You are an idiot	He is listening to me
That's not bad	That's good	That's poor
That is a very brave proposal	You are insane	He thinks I have courage
Quite good	A bit disappointing	Quite good
I would suggest	Do it or be prepared to justify yourself	Think about the idea, but do what you like
Oh, incidentally/by the way	The primary purpose of our discussion is	That is not very important
I was a bit disappointed that	I am annoyed that	It doesn't really matter
Very interesting	That is clearly nonsense	They are impressed
I'll bear it in mind	I've forgotten it already	They will probably do it
I'm sure it's my fault	It's your fault	Why do they think it was their fault?
You must come for dinner	It's not an invitation, I'm just being polite	I will get an invitation soon
I almost agree	I don't agree at all	He's not far from agreement
I only have a few minor comments	Please rewrite completely	He has found a few typos
Could we consider some other options	I don't like your idea	They have not yet decided

I have found sharing this type of teaching with small group leaders and, as necessary, as part of welcome courses to be important pastorally. We do need to support those suffering from culture shock, to help them understand the different stages and encourage them to normalise their feelings. We need to support people emotionally and spiritually. To understand their perspective. We also need to encourage our people not to be judgemental of those suffering from culture shock.

In addition to understanding culture shock, it is worth looking at how national cultures differ. The standard work on this is by Gert and Geert Hofstede and their work on cultural dimensions.[49]

Hofstede's cultural dimensions

Hofstede is a Dutch academic who did work for IBM to help them understand their workforce in different nations, and how the culture of a nation impacted and interfaced with the overall IBM culture. He originally identified four dimensions of culture to which a further two were added later. These dimensions are very helpful when we seek to understand where people from different nations are coming from when they join our churches.

One dimension is **power distance**. The extent to which workers feel equal to their bosses and the implications this has for other hierarchical relationships. The following grid compares typical characteristics of societies with small and high-power distances.[50]

---

49. Geert Hofstede, Gert Jan Hofstede, *Cultures and Organizations* (New York: McGraw-Hill, 2005). Permission received
50. Hofstede and Hofstede, *Cultures and Organizations*, p. 59.

Small Power Distance	High Power Distance
Inequalities minimised	Inequalities expected and desires
Parents treat children as equals	Parents teach children obedience
Students treat teachers as equals	Students give teachers respect, even outside class
Teachers expect initiative from students	Teachers take initiative
There are fewer supervisors	More supervisors
Subordinates expect to be consulted	Subordinates expect to be told what to do
Privilege and status symbols are frowned upon	Privilege and status symbols are normal and popular
Power is based on formal position, expertise, and ability to give rewards	Power is based on tradition or family, charisma, and the ability to use force
All should have equal rights	The powerful should have privileges
Politics about dialogue	Politics has elements of violence
Less corruption and scandals end careers	Scandals covered up
Small income differences in society	Large income differences in society
Greater democracy	Autocratic government

Hierarchical relationships exist in churches, either in perception or reality. Hofstede proposes that the extent of power differences can differ between nations and therefore there can be vastly different expectations based on the perceived hierarchy from different members of the congregation. Using Hofstede's research, we see that the UK, USA, Holland and Germany have low power distances. Nigeria and India have some of the highest. So, the UK, USA, Holland and Germany sit on the left of the above grid, Nigeria and India on the right.

This can impact the extent that members of a congregation expect to be told what to do by those in leadership rather than be consulted. Nigerians and Indians expect to be told, while those from the UK expect to be consulted. It can also impact the types of sermon people expect. Those from Nigerian and Indian cultures might expect more directional sermons rather than sermons encouraging the congregation to think for themselves and make their own judgements. How leaders will be viewed will also be impacted. People from some cultures will want to call me pastor or another title of honour; they will struggle to treat me as a peer. I have concluded that if someone wants to honour me and call me pastor, I need to accept that; however, I know of others who resist it.

It is helpful to be aware of these different viewpoints and recognise how the way we view things can be due to the culture we are used to. We all need to compare our cultural predisposition with what the Bible teaches and learn from each other.

Another dimension in Hofstede's work is **individual versus corporate**. The extent to which people feel their own sense of identity versus being part of a group. We have already mentioned regularly the impact of the Western individualistic view of the world.[51]

---

51. Hofstede and Hofstede, *Cultures and Organizations*, p. 109.

Corporate	Individual
People born into extended families	Everyone grows up to look after themselves and immediate family only
Children learn to think in we	Children learn to think in I
Harmony maintained; confrontations avoided	Speaking one's mind is characteristic of an honest person
Friendships are predetermined	Friendships are voluntary
Resources shared with relatives	Individual ownership
Social network primary source of information	Media primary source of information
Students only speak up when asked	Individuals expected to speak for themselves
Qualifications provide access to higher status groups	Qualifications increase wealth and self-respect
Hiring and firing take your group into account	Hiring and firing based on rules and skills only
Relationship more important than task	Task more important than relationship
Opinions based on what the group thinks	Everyone expected to have their own opinion
Group interests outweigh those of the individual	Individual interests most important
Private life invaded by groups	Everyone has the right to privacy

This again can impact how church life is viewed. The UK is seen as an outlier on this index too, being one of the most individualistic societies alongside the USA. Nigeria is again at the other end of the continuum, being highly corporate. South Africa and India are mid-point.

I experienced conflict with a Nigerian member of my team because I did not fully understand this dynamic. He gave a higher value to relationships than me and other members of the team. We felt we had a good relationship and focused on task. He struggled with this and didn't feel part of the team. Every time he joined a gathering, even if he was late, he would personally greet everyone. At that stage our culture wasn't such that these things could be discussed; we were unable to learn from each other. We missed God's best for our leadership and for the church.

This dynamic isn't just relevant at a leadership level. Many ethnic minorities from a culture that values the corporate over the individual are used to a depth of community and fellowship that is missing in many of our churches. We have much to learn from them, but also recognise their struggles within our individualistic society.

I have also discovered that people from some cultures are unlikely to contribute to a discussion unless they are invited to do so. I am also now aware of my instinct to take relationship for granted and to prioritise task.

We must appreciate everyone and learn from them. Doing so creates a much healthier team dynamic.

The third contrast proposed is between **feminine and masculine** societies, the different gender roles.[52]

---

52. Hofstede and Hofstede, *Cultures and Organizations*, p. 132.

Feminine	Masculine
Relationships and quality of life important	Challenge, earnings, recognition, and advancement important
Both boys and girls are allowed to cry	Girls cry, boys don't; boys fight back, girls don't
Bridegrooms and brides are held to the same standards	Brides need to be chaste and industrious, grooms don't
Mothers and fathers deal with facts and feelings	Mothers deal with feelings, fathers deal with facts
Same norm for male and female nudity	Stronger taboo for male nudity
Women's liberation about equal shares at home and work	Women admitted to positions previously reserved for men
Competitive sport outside of school	Competitive sport within school
Women and men shop for food and cars	Women shop for food, men for cars
Couples share a car	Couples need two cars
Conflict is resolved by compromise and negotiation	Conflict resolved by the strongest winning
People work to live	People live to work
Immigrants should integrate	Immigrants should assimilate
Politics about coalitions working together	Politics about mudslinging

Again, it should be stressed that this is about society as a whole and not about churches in a nation, so not all of these apply. However, it is helpful as the general culture we are part of does impact the church. In this case the UK, USA and India are strongly masculine, Nigeria is mid-point with Holland an outlier, being strongly feminine.

This is another area where we need to wisely seek to hear what the Bible says and to recognise the perspective of those from a different culture, rather than follow our culture. We need to humbly hear other points of view and seek to learn from each other.

There are movements that would encourage the church to be more masculine, to display more of the attributes on the right-hand side, to be able to attract more men from our society. The question we need to ask is not what works but what does God want? Personally, I find the above list challenging as I naturally incline to the characteristics on the right but am aware that many of those on the left are closer to what I find in Scripture.

The fourth and final contrast is our **attitude to uncertainty**. Uncertainty avoidance has nothing to do with risk avoidance, nor with following rules. It has to do with anxiety and distrust in the face of the unknown, and conversely, with a wish to have fixed habits and rituals, and to know the truth.[53]

---

53. Hofstede and Hofstede, *Cultures and Organizations*, p. 176.

Weak uncertainty avoidance	Strong uncertainty avoidance
Low stress and low anxiety	High stress and high anxiety
Aggression and emotions should not be shown	Aggression and emotions may at proper times and places be vented
Comfortable in ambiguous situations and with unfamiliar tasks	Fear of ambiguous situations and unfamiliar tasks
What is different is curious	What is different is dangerous
Lenient rules for children on what is dirty or taboo	Firm rules for children on what is dirty or taboo
More heart attacks	Less heart attacks
More nurses, fewer doctors	More doctors, fewer nurses
Teachers can say I don't know	Teachers need all the answers
Used cars and DIY	New cars and home repairs by experts
People change jobs frequently	Longer service
No more rules than strictly necessary	Emotional need for rules, even if they do not work
Tolerance, even of extreme ideas	Repression of extremism
Few general or unwritten rules	Many and precise rules and unwritten rules
Ethnic tolerance	Ethnic prejudice
Religious truth should not be imposed on others	Only one truth and we have it
Nobody should be persecuted for their beliefs	Religious, political intolerance and fundamentalism

Once again, the UK is at an extreme, along with the USA, and Nigeria and India they are on the left of the above table. Other European nations such as France and Spain are intolerant of uncertainty and are more strongly on the right.

This is another area that impacts church life – how dogmatic should we be? It also shows that people from some cultures will find multicultural church with is ambiguities easier than others.

We need to understand that people come from different perspectives, which need to be compared to the Word of God.

This inevitably has been a very quick overview of the impact of culture and the need for us to understand it and its impact on churches. It is especially important for those who are called to lead multicultural churches.

In the following chapters, we will build on this by looking at things from the perspective of different minorities that might be in our churches, different types of 'mice' and what we can learn from them.

Questions to ponder

- How can we move from gathering people from other cultures to getting to know them and learning from them?
- Are you aware of culture shock? Have you seen symptoms of it within yourself or others within your congregation?
- Have you experience of tensions because of the clash of cultures within your congregation?

8.

Understanding Things from a Minority Perspective

As noted earlier, when an elephant and a mouse are in a room together, the mouse is motivated to learn everything about the elephant for self-preservation. The elephant doesn't have the same felt need. If we are to create diverse churches with differences celebrated as God-given, the majority culture, the elephant, must understand not just about culture generally, but also the perspective of the minority culture, the mouse.

Tim Keller observes this from an American perspective:

> In short, nearly every racial minority in the US understands Euro-white culture pretty well, but we whites are far more ignorant of how the cultures of others operate ... That means that in mixed race churches, the burden of relationship maintenance tends to fall disproportionately on racial minorities, even if they are well represented statistically.[54]

---

54. Irwyn L. Ince Jr, *The Beautiful Community: Unity, Diversity, and the Church at its Best* (Westmont, IL: IVP, 2020), Kindle Android version, p. 2.

In this chapter I share insights I have gleaned from other ethnicities, which I hope will highlight other perspectives and therefore help us move towards more inclusive communities.

Challenges people face

Gathering people of different ethnicities to our churches isn't the most difficult thing, as for many of those coming to our nation from the Caribbean and from Africa, church is part of their life and heritage. It is helping newcomers fully feel part of the whole, not just observers, that is hard.

We must therefore understand the barriers that minorities have in feeling integrated and fully included in white majority churches. Many people from minority backgrounds struggle to feel accepted in society as a whole, and can therefore have a mindset that they will not be fully accepted as equals in white majority churches and white-led churches. With the upsurge of concern in our country about recent levels of immigration, this is a particular and important challenge.

We therefore must recognise that there are barriers that must be overcome.

Glenn Bracey, a sociology professor who is also a black evangelical Christian, published an academic paper based on research he personally conducted by being part of seven predominantly white churches in the USA.[55]

In being part of these churches over several years, he was seeking to find out why churches continue to be racially segregated, despite saying they want to be racially diverse.

---

55. www.researchgate.net/publication/316355727_Race_Tests_Racial_Boundary_Maintenance_in_White_Evangelical_Churches (accessed 10.10.24).

His conclusion was that unconscious, semi-permeable membranes exist that keep the churches mostly white. These membranes are created by key people within the church, especially leaders. (While his research was among white churches in the USA, his conclusions appear relevant in the UK for both white churches wanting to attract non-whites and black churches wanting to attract white people.)

The barriers or membranes he found leaders create include tailoring services to attract white, middle-class congregants. By this he meant the style of preaching, music, length of services, structure of services, dress codes, political and community activities, missionary interests and theological emphases are consistent with white religious traditions or tailored to reach 'unchurched' whites; having positive attitudes about whites and negative views of people of colour, discursive techniques for justifying racial inequality and priorities that favour whites' material and emotional interests.

Some indictment! It certainly gives food for thought for us all and is a challenge. Not all will be valid, but it is a good checklist to use to consider how ethnic minorities might view your services and your church.

He also talks about his experience of an exaggerated initial welcome for potential congregants of colour. However, if they seemed to challenge the normative boundaries of white privilege and power within the space, they were less welcome! He sometimes felt he wasn't accepted for who he was as an individual but as a generic black man. For example, in one church he was asked to be in the worship group, despite his gifts being elsewhere. He observed that 'white evangelical ministers often attempt to increase membership by placing people of colour in highly visible positions as worship leaders, to predictably mixed results when used as a "quick fix".'[56] In another church, before they even got to know him, he was asked to mentor a mixed-race youngster who did not have a father figure, even though the absent father was obviously white. He concluded: 'In each case, the warm welcome was preconditioned by white evangelicals' perceived need for a new person of colour to play a particular racialized role in the white space.'[57]

His general conclusion is that he felt the white leaders involved were not aware of the impact they were having: 'They never showed any obvious signs of anger or frustration with our presence.'[58] However, the result of all this is that the churches remained predominantly white; people of colour intuitively felt they were not really wanted.

Ben Lindsay comes from a second-generation Jamaican background. He became a leader in a white majority church. He shares some of his experiences and observations in his book *We Need to Talk About Race*.[59] It is a book worth reading. He too raises concerns about ethnic minorities feeling 'othered', treated as a stereotype representative of their ethnic community. That happens regularly in the mainstream media; it can also be experienced in the church.[60]

These are not easy things to overcome; however, we need to put in the hard work to address them; to help people see

---

56. www.researchgate.net/publication/316355727_Race_Tests_Racial_Boundary_Maintenance_in_White_Evangelical_Churches p. 289 (accessed 11.11.24).
57. As above (accessed 11.11.24).
58. www.researchgate.net/publication/316355727_Race_Tests_Racial_Boundary_Maintenance_in_White_Evangelical_Churches p. 291 (accessed 11.11.24).
59. Ben Lindsay, *We Need To Talk About Race: Understanding the Black Experience in White Majority Churches* (London: SPCK, 2019), Kindle edition.
60. Lindsay, *We Need To Talk About Race*, Kindle location 460.

beyond stereotypes; to be thoughtful of how our humour and off-hand remarks can be heard by others; to understand how we make visitors who are different from the majority culture feel. The examples given are where white is the majority culture, but the principle is the same if the majority are Jamaican or Ghanaian.

My friend and colleague Linda Geevanathan, whose family background is Sri Lankan, shared her experience with me:

> When my family first got saved and started going to church, early on we went to a church in Darwin, Australia, and I remember cringing every time we would walk into the main hall. Not only were we one of the few families from an ethnic background, but for myself, I was aware of how my family stood out like a sore thumb. That was more than twenty-five years ago, but to be perfectly honest, my experience of church here in the UK has not been that much better. I found to survive in the family of churches I was a part of, I had to assimilate to the majority culture, and in this process, I struggled to celebrate my own culture and tragically lost some of what was most precious about it.
>
> If only as a newly saved teenager someone had told me that my culture was not something to be looked down on or seen as lesser, but rather that my mum bringing samosas to church instead of cake like everybody else was not just OK but a gift to be valued and celebrated! If only I had seen leaders in the church from other nations. I saw it out in the secular world but in the church, the place where I should have belonged more than any other, I saw no place for someone like

me. The irony was that we often sang of God reaching the nations – but what did we mean? Are we really ready for multicultural church here in the UK? Or do we want multiracial church, where the minority assimilate into the common culture? Assimilation isn't messy, it isn't uncomfortable, not for the majority – but for those of us from the minority, like me, it can be soul destroying.

My journey over the last few years has been a revelation; it has been healing and releasing. I am learning what it looks like to lead as myself. My culture, my personality and my perspective. Layers of self-doubt and damage to the very heart of who I am have been stripped away and healed.

If we really want to be a multicultural church, it is not simply about skin tone, but about the intentional engagement of cultures. To truly reflect the heart of God as a church, we will not simply have people from many different nations or backgrounds in our congregations, but we will engage to some degree with each of their cultural contexts. We will have to put to death the arrogance that says our way, our culture is the best, and learn in humility what it looks like to honour and celebrate all cultures – including our own.

My heart will smile the first time I walk into a church and there at the end of the service are samosas, not because of a special occasion, not as a one-off event, but just because once every few weeks there are samosas. Trivial it may appear, but to the heart of someone like me, it is an everyday act of acknowledgement, honour and celebration.[61]

From this we see the challenge for minorities to keep their cultural accent; it is so much easier to assimilate. It took Linda a long time before she felt confident enough to share her true feelings, to trust me enough to be open. To what extent is this true for people in your congregation – how would you even know? I find listening to the experiences of Linda and others like her deeply moving, and it challenges me to believe that we just must do better.

As Ben Lindsay shares:

> Too often minority groups have shied away from expressing the reality of their experiences because they do not want to come across as victims. They do not want to be defined by those experiences and they tire of defending themselves to majority groups who accuse them of self-indulgent navel gazing, and question whether their views, experiences or struggles are real.[62]

We need to seek to create an atmosphere of trust such that people are willing to tell us how they really feel. To do this we need to publicly give permission for people to share how they feel without fear of judgement; we also need to create safe places privately, in our relationships with people, for them to share.

---

61. Edited for the purposes of this book.
62. Lindsay, *We Need To Talk About Race*, Kindle edition, p. 19.

Other attitudes within white culture that are off-putting to minorities

My reading and discussions with ethnic minorities who are part of predominantly white churches has identified several elements that they struggle with.

These include white people being unaware of their privileges. For example, I have never had to worry about what to wear because I might be racially profiled by the police or be a victim of mistaken identity. I have never had the sense that my physical presence is a threat to women, who automatically cross the road or hold tight to their handbags on approach. I take it for granted that there will be positive images of my ethnicity in books, films and art. I expect people who look like me to be in the highest employment and leadership positions. I am unaware of the negative impact the lack of positive role models have on the children who do not look like me, and therefore the need of ethnic parents to overcompensate. In short, I can be unaware of my privilege.

What people from minority cultures talk about and what the majority culture talk about can be different. Black majority churches readily speak on issues that affect their community, such as youth violence, unemployment, financial struggles, while white majority churches tend to speak more broadly on issues of 'the human condition', often neglecting to acknowledge the disproportionate struggles that minorities face.

The priorities of some white churches are very different from the priorities of people from ethnic minorities. Numerical church growth, slick worship, generic social action programmes, a cool website and overseas mission/

church planting can be seen in opposition to making local connections, listening to the needs of local families and developing projects/programmes in partnership with the local community, which feel more of a priority to ethnic minorities. While most Christians believe the church can be a major force for societal and structural change, they miss the fact that to be effective we are going to need to engage with and listen to the very people who are suffering injustice.

These insights need to be heard. Injustices in our society disproportionately impact minorities; if we ignore them, that gives a message that either we don't care, or they are unimportant. Neither is a message we should not be giving. When we listen to others, it can challenge our understanding of the kingdom and realign our point of view, making it less egocentric.

The challenges of releasing minority leaders

Many people are coming to the UK as missionaries, yet we can sometimes struggle to distinguish them from economic migrants. God is sending partners to work with us; we need to learn how to make the best use of the gifts God is sending us.

It is crucial for there to be a greater breadth of leadership within our churches, for our leadership to be diverse, as well as our congregations. The lack of senior black leadership in white-led, black majority churches is known in the black community as the 'Guinness effect'– white majority leadership on top, black majority employees or congregation at the bottom. However, bringing black leaders through within white-led contexts has its own challenges.

Ben Lindsay didn't feel his perspective was valued and was even ridiculed:

> When I studied at theological college, I felt like we were speaking about two different worlds and that was largely because the institution did not seem open to my understanding of God – rooted in black and Pentecostal perspectives it didn't seem welcome at the table. I often felt like black Pentecostal Christians were the butt of theological humour ... I felt 'othered' – it was actually my awakening to the conversation of race and Christianity.[63]

Minorities in leadership in predominantly white contexts talk about feeling too white for black people and too black for white people, therefore feeling isolated and lonely. This isolation, coupled with subtle micro-aggressions from white people and the tightness of the structure and organisation which is alien to black culture, can cause stresses, can cause burnout, and many bow out.

Leading multicultural teams is also challenging for those from the majority culture.

Speaking personally, I have found leading a multicultural leadership team challenging, but also fulfilling. I have had to come to terms with the reality that discussing topics and arriving at decisions is harder and takes much longer than if everyone is from the same background. White British leaders expect the meetings to be logical, with a presentation of topics, discussion and then decisions. Ethnic minority leaders expect a more spiritual approach, with topics soaked in

---

63. Lindsay, *We Need To Talk About Race*, Kindle edition, p. 100.

prayer prior to a decision being reached. I have found this emphasis helpful; prayer became a more significant part of our leadership meetings. I tried to ensure that there was a pattern of every other leadership meeting being prayer focused. Even this was a challenge, and often our business-led culture crept into the time dedicated to prayer.

White leaders tend to be concise and assertive, sometimes even imposing and disdainful of others. In contrast, others will not be straightforward, telling a long story hoping that others will grasp their opinion through the story. I found that I need to exercise strong leadership in drawing out some to express their opinion, which will not be forthcoming unless asked, while trying to stop others from dominating.

We need to give real thought and consideration to how leaders from minority cultures experience leadership teams and how the teams are led; it is not easy. I have made so many mistakes and have had to reflect and ask for forgiveness on many occasions. The benefits far outweigh the downsides.

Worship and preaching styles

This is another key area where we need to hear the perspective of others.

I interviewed members of the church I led about their perspective on the church.[64] What was mentioned frequently was the challenge of a different worship style. This is the experience of many.

Israel Olofinjana is a Nigerian missionary sent to the UK to plant a Nigerian Pentecostal church in London. However,

---

64. https://youtu.be/ha29Jqmin9M?si=G40X_29DqbAoRb3S (accessed 9.10.24).

instead he found himself leading a multicultural Baptist church. He found there were many Nigerian churches in London, but none attracted white people. He therefore decided to abandon his church plant to join an existing British church. This caused some initial problems with his sending pastor, but he carried on anyway! His is an interesting story.[65] Israel describes the biggest challenge he found was in worship style, which, compared to the exuberant style of African Pentecostal worship, felt like a cemetery!

Other African leaders in predominantly white churches, such as Kenyan Peter Oyugi, say the same thing, adding that the change in worship style is costly for other Africans, and has prevented some from joining the church they lead.[66]

I believe we need to create space to talk openly about worship styles at both leadership and congregational levels, for people to recognise that we all have our own preferred worship style and sometimes our favourite worship leader. Yet worship isn't just about our preferences and, contrary to the opinion of some, a particular worship style is not more biblical than another. When we worship in the age to come, we will be transfixed by the one we are worshipping rather than how we worship! We need to allow for a wide range of styles in the meantime.

Within my context, it has taken a long time for worship leaders to come through to lead, and even longer for them to feel confident enough to lead in their own cultural style alongside the traditional style we have been used to. One Jamaican leader in our church introduced us to the worship style she grew up with, energetically playing the tambourine;

---

65. Olofinjana, ed., *Turning the Tables on Mission*, Kindle location 1982.
66. Olofinjana, ed., *Turning the Tables on Mission*, Kindle location 2426.

using a combination of old hymns and simple repetitive choruses was fantastic and embraced by all. Similarly, an African family, husband, wife and two young boys leading us in worship with just their voices and drums has also enhanced our worship experience as a church. However, they had been leading for a long time before they felt confident and released to bring a different style of worship to us.

Preaching is another area in which we can benefit from listening to the input of minority groups. We need to hear from them in both preaching content as well as style. For example, many Africans bring an awareness of spiritual forces that we have lost in the West. Some have direct experiences of the supernatural and witchdoctors, and they recognise clearly the importance of proclaiming the lordship of Christ over all things. They recognise that this is at least as important and relevant as where you go when you die. Other cultures bring an understanding of the liberation motif in Scripture and other biblical themes less emphasised in Western Christianity. We can and should learn from each other.

I tend to preach in a typical Western linear style; however, I appreciate that there is great value in other styles. I value what I call the 'impressionist' style of preaching that will paint a picture by using lots of different points that together make a whole. This will include lots of digressions. Other preachers are naturally much more emotional in their preaching than me. They use changes in voice tone, sometimes shouting, sometimes crying, using repetition to make a point. I have had to work hard to release others to preach in their own style rather than to seek to emulate me. I have learned so much from preachers from other cultures; maybe they have even learned something from me. The appreciation and release of different preaching styles needs to be a clear focus or it will not happen and takes time, but adds variety and introduces us to different ways of hearing from God.

For many, worship and preaching styles are not things we give as much thought to as we should; clearly there are things we can learn from one another. Again, I have found it helpful to create contexts where we can discuss these things together in a safe place, to allow the input from ethnic leaders to challenge us in these areas.

I find it sobering listening to the perspectives of my brothers and sisters in Christ when they share their personal experiences, which they rarely do due to fears of rejection. It is so important that we hear what they say and seek to respond and create a safe, welcoming place for them. Listening to the perspectives of others and then releasing them in leadership among us without them feeling they need to adapt to our cultural style is an even greater blessing.

Questions to ponder

- How can we treat everyone as an individual, seeing beyond their ethnicity?
- How can we create safe places so that minorities can share honestly about their experiences in the church and wider society?
- Are you comfortable with styles that are not your preference? How can you encourage, enable and develop those who bring a different way of doing things, so that the congregation can learn from other ways of doing things?

9.

Justice

I hope I have made the case that to reach the UK, we need to learn how to be truly multicultural, which means we need to be willing to learn from other cultures; to stand in other people's shoes. We have seen that when an elephant is in the room with a mouse, the mouse is motivated to understand the elephant, while the elephant has no intrinsic need to learn about the mouse. For Isaiah's vision of a wolf lying down with the lamb to be fulfilled, the wolf needs to give up its privilege and protect the lamb, and the lamb must learn to trust the wolf. Those with power need to decide to learn more about those less powerful and no longer be a threat to them.

Historical issues of injustice, including those perpetrated by Christians and the church, are strongly felt by many minorities today. Many white Western Christians find this hard to understand, partly because we are less acquainted with our history. For some the issue is slavery, but for most it is colonisation. This is a crucial area that the majority need to listen to the minority about. Past injustices make it challenging for the lamb to live with the wolf!

The legacy of slavery and colonisation

Ben Lindsay, from a Jamaican background but brought up in London, explains:

> While it's fair to say that black people in the UK are no longer in chains, there is an assumption that past historic events, such as the transatlantic slave trade, have left no apparent scars on subsequent black generations, as if to say the damage caused has no impact on our present.[67]

He obviously disagrees with that assumption. He and other Caribbean friends talk about the injustice they feel with regards to how Britain spent £20 million, 40 per cent of our national budget, to buy the freedom of slaves in 1833. For many of British heritage, that would seem like we did a good thing as a nation. The perceived injustice stems from the fact that the money was borrowed, and the national debt wasn't paid off until 2015. Therefore, Ben's parents and grandparents were paying taxes to compensate slave owners who enslaved their ancestors. No money was given to the ex-slaves.

This sense of injustice in paying taxes to compensate rich slave owners grates because of the perceived disparities in living standards of different communities having roots in

---

67. Lindsay, *We Need To Talk About Race*, p. 65.

historical injustices. Many of my Caribbean friends feel their community is still impoverished compared to many others in the UK, and trace that back to the legacy of slavery, hence the call for reparations. We should not underestimate the strength of feeling our brothers and sisters in Christ feel about this, something many Christians are unaware of.

For those from an African and Asian background, injustice is not around issues of slavery but about the impact of colonisation and its links with Western missions. This is Harvey Kwiyani, an academic working in the UK and originally from Malawi, as mentioned earlier; he bluntly explains the legacy of the perceived role of the church in colonisation: 'In the eyes of those in the majority world there seemed to be little distinction between Western missionaries, traders and colonial agents.'[68]

He talks about how by the middle of the last century, the Western missionary movement was rejected because it was felt that mission and colonisation were seen as two sides of the same coin. Missionaries were seen as partners with colonial agents in an attempt to dominate the world. He makes his point with reference to the father of missions, William Carey: 'Carey referred to the millions of uncivilized "pagans" and "Mohammedans", reflecting the paternalistic tones with which Western Christians spoke of the rest of the world at the time.'[69]

The independence movements across Africa wasn't therefore just about freedom from colonial political rule, but also for freedom from missionary rule within the churches. Kwiyani says:

---

68. Kwiyani, *Multicultural Kingdom,* p. 24. Permission received.
69. Kwiyani, *Multicultural Kingdom,* p. 29. Permission received.

In the 1960s the emerging churches of the majority world (wrongly labelled 'younger churches') started to agitate for independence for their countries both from colonial rule and from Western missionaries in favour of indigenous Christian leadership in their countries ... indigenous leaders were arguing for the decolonization of the missionary churches both in sub-Saharan Africa and in the wider non-Western world. 'Missionaries, go home!' became the rallying cry, as many wanted to be free from missionary influence.[70]

This view is shocking for many and not something most Christians are aware of. It is not something I was aware of until recently. It is important that we understand where many of our brothers and sisters in Christ are coming from, as it still impacts relationships.

This perspective of colonisation being linked with the church is endorsed by Brazilian missions' commentator Analzira Nascimento. She has written about the unhealthy recent impact on missions into Brazil, and then goes on to suggest that Brazilians are now making the same mistake as they take the gospel around the world. This is important as Brazil is one of the biggest contributors to missions around the world, including to the UK.[71]

The impact of colonisation therefore casts a big shadow for many on the church today; the white church being implicated in historical injustices without us being aware of

---

70. Kwiyani, *Multicultural Kingdom*, p. 39. Permission received.
71. Analzira Nascimento, *Evangelization or Colonization? (Global Voices: Latin America)* (Oxford: Regnum Books International, 2021), Kindle edition.

it; the white church being regarded with a level of suspicion and creating another barrier so that many from ethnic backgrounds feel uncomfortable in predominantly white churches. Being aware of this legacy enables us to address it where possible and necessary.

Learning from Martin Luther King about the impact of racism

Despite coming from a very different context, I have found *The Letter From Birmingham Jail* by Martin Luther King very helpful. Maybe it is because it is from a different context, and the injustice of American racism in the 1960s is widely understood, that enables it to be helpful. I have known of this long letter, which has been published in book form, for some time. It is regularly quoted by others, but until recently I had not read it. I am so glad I now have and would encourage you to do the same. It helped me grasp what it is like to be the victim of racism and injustice, which many people in our nation are, and how the white church is implicated.

The letter was originally written while King was in jail in 1963 for disturbing the peace. He had been leading peaceful demonstrations against racial segregation in America. He wrote the letter on the margins of a newspaper, and it was smuggled out of prison. It was written to and in response to six white church leaders who were saying the protests should stop and the battle should be fought in the courts, not the streets. King's insights are articulate, profound and still relevant, as injustice is still prevalent in our society and felt by many people from different cultures.

He explains the basic problem: 'Lamentably, it is an historical fact that privileged groups seldom give up their privileges voluntarily.'[72] A profound thought, which explains why inequalities in society are so difficult to get rid of. White churches, not just white people, are seen by many as privileged groups, still having the same privileges they had in the colonial era and unwilling to give them up.

King paints the picture of what injustice feels like for the victim, helping his readers to place themselves in someone else's shoes. He draws comparisons with how different nations across the globe are receiving their independence, while blacks in the US have been waiting 340 years for their God-given rights. He decries the white church leaders who suggest that he should wait for the courts to pronounce while lynch mobs still patrol the streets, and 'hate-filled policemen' attack his brothers and sisters on a whim. He decries the poverty of the black man in the middle of an affluent society. He concludes by asking people to think about how he feels, trying to explain to his daughter why she cannot go to the fun park because she is a person of colour, and to see her unconsciously developing a bitterness towards white people.[73]

What King describes is different from our context. However, I have found that I can easily ignore injustices until I get an insight into what it means to be a victim of them. Many of the cultures around us are in some sense victims of both historical and current injustices. It is easy to dismiss this. The

---

72. Martin Luther King, *Letter From Birmingham Jail* (London: Penguin Randon House, 1964, 2018), p. 7.
73. King, *Letter From Birmingham Jail*, p. 8.

number of times I have heard people being told they have a chip on their shoulder when they talk about their experience of injustice! If we want reconciliation, we must listen.

Another interesting insight is that he feels he is standing in the middle of two opposing forces in the black community: 'One is a force of complacency, made up in part of Negroes who, as a result of long years of oppression, are so drained of self-respect ... that they have adjusted to segregation ... The other force is one of bitterness and hatred, and it comes perilously close to advocating violence.'[74]

I am sure this polarisation is true in any community that is the victim of injustice. My Muslim friends especially tell me this is one of their challenges. Our nation and most of the world are rightly concerned about terrorism, particularly terrorism in the name of Islam. Various initiatives are being put forward by society as ways to combat it, many of which could be seen as curtailing the freedom of Muslims to practise their faith. Examples include proposed legislation which requires faith groups teaching children for more than six hours a week to be Ofsted inspected; schools having to raise concerns with authorities if they perceive children are being indoctrinated by religious groups. There is polarisation in the Muslim community about this; everyone I know condemns terrorism and voices clearly that it is not true Islam. The action being taken itself causes problems; as King says, some react with anger and it makes the situation far worse; on the other hand, many are so beaten down they just shrug their shoulders and get on with life, but have a deep resentment towards the majority population.

---

74. King, *Letter From Birmingham Jail*, pp. 16-17.

Understanding these tensions within the Muslim community is important as we seek to build relationships with them. These tensions are strong among Muslims but also exist with other communities in the UK, at a lesser level, but they are there. We need to be aware of this.

King's critique of white liberals and the white church is something else needing reflection; am I, are we, guilty of the same thing? I think we are! He proclaims that the biggest stumbling block to freedom for blacks is not the Ku Klux Klan but the white moderate who puts order as more important than justice. This was clearly directed at the white pastors who had publicly challenged him to take the battle off the streets and into the court rooms, to whom he addressed the letter. He declared: 'Shallow understanding from people of good will is more frustrating than absolute misunderstanding from people of ill will. Lukewarm acceptance is much more bewildering than outright rejection.'[75] He bluntly summarises, 'I have been so greatly disappointed with the white church and its leadership.'

I have concluded that if I want to build a true multicultural church, I need to be willing to speak out for justice. In doing so, I have faced criticism from white friends, but I have concluded this is a price worth paying. Our church publicly declares that it speaks out against discrimination and seeks to put that into practice.

As Christians, we are rightly concerned whenever our freedom of expression of our faith is being curtailed. However, I can't get away from the famous quote attributed

---

75. King, *Letter From Birmingham Jail*, p. 13.

to Martin Niemöller regarding life in Germany in the 1930s and 1940s:

> First they came for the Communists, but I was not a Communist so I did not speak out. Then they came for the Socialists and the Trade Unionists, but I was neither, so I did not speak out. Then they came for the Jews, but I was not a Jew so I did not speak out. And when they came for me, there was no one left to speak out for me.[76]

I believe that as Christians we must speak out strongly for our right to exercise our faith in the UK and across the world. There are examples in the UK where Christians are stopped from expressing their sincerely held Christian principles. We should speak out against this discrimination. The treatment of Christians in some countries around the world is outrageous and we should be outraged and speak out against it. Interestingly, many Muslims I know are also outraged by the treatment of Christians in some countries that claim to be Islamic. However, we need to not just speak out for justice for ourselves, but for everyone. That is at the heart of the gospel.

King lays down the challenge of what he says the church should be like:

> There was a time when the church was very powerful – in the time when the early Christians rejoiced at being deemed worthy to suffer for what they believed. In those

---

76. www.jewishvirtuallibrary.org/martin-niemoeller-the-failure-to-speak-up-against-the-nazis (accessed 9.10. 24).

days the church was not merely a thermometer that recorded the ideas and principles of popular opinion; it was a thermostat that transformed the mores of society ... If today's church does not recapture the sacrificial spirit of the early church it will lose its authenticity, forfeit the loyalty of millions, and be dismissed as an irrelevant social club with no meaning for the twentieth century.[77]

Ben Lindsay thinks the reason why the white church is declining is as King predicted: 'I believe the failure of the white-led, white majority churches in diverse communities to communicate the God of justice has contributed to the decline of the traditional church and the increase in membership of the black church.'[78]

Those of us who have greater privilege should use that not just to speak up for ourselves, but on behalf of others. This calls for a measure of sacrifice, but I would suggest in the larger picture of things, not a big sacrifice. Those who feel themselves victims are watching us; a failure to do so creates barriers that are very difficult to overcome, whether we are seeking to build relationships with Christians from different backgrounds or with Muslims.

King then goes on to respond to the accusation of being an extremist. He says he has gained a measure of satisfaction from the label, saying it groups him with other extremists! Such as Jesus, an extremist for love; Amos, an extremist for justice; Paul, an extremist for the gospel. Martin Luther,

---

77. King, *Letter From Birmingham Jail*, p. 24.
78. Lindsay, *We Need To Talk About Race*, p. 155.

John Bunyan, Abraham Lincoln and Thomas Jefferson are other extremists he would seek to emulate. He says, 'The question is not whether we will be extremists, but what kind of extremists we will be. Will we be extremists for hate or for love?'[79]

There is such a challenge here for the church today, especially the church of privilege; will we be sacrificial, or will we become maintainers of the status quo? Will we put ourselves in the shoes of victims of injustice and understand what it feels like from their perspective? What sort of extremist will we be? Will we be relevant or irrelevant? I have concluded to be fully multicultural is to be an extremist!

Martin Luther King's wisdom is such that more than fifty years later, it still speaks to me. I have found his wisdom crucial as I have sought to lead a church of many different cultures.

If we are to put ourselves in the shoes of brothers and sisters in Christ from other nations and cultures, we will become more passionate for justice, seeking to learn from and acknowledging past mistakes. Unless we do so, there will still be great suspicion of the 'white church'. In doing so, we will face criticism from those who will dismiss us as buying into a 'woke' agenda. We are not, we are following a God of justice; we are doing what Jesus did and would do!

---

79. King, *Letter From Birmingham Jail*, p. 19.

Questions to ponder

- How can we create opportunities where the feelings of victims of injustice can be openly expressed?
- How might you and your church speak out against injustice?
- What sort of extremist do you want to be?

10.

Reading the Bible with Blinkers Removed

Despite being a Christian for many years, one of the revelations I have had only recently is how easily we can read the Bible through our cultural perspective. As we read, our prejudices are confirmed rather than challenged.

In relation to the subject of this book, from time immemorial, humans have held prejudices against others based on their ethnicity, the colour of their skin, or factors such as where they are from and how they speak. We are all guilty of it, and I believe it is best to recognise it so that we can do something about it. I would suggest it even impacts how we read the Bible and understand its message.

Engaging with other cultural perspectives is therefore important in broadening our understanding and revealing our blind spots. This has been a wonderful byproduct of my friendships with people from different backgrounds. In this chapter I share some of the ways my understanding of the Bible has changed through the influence and insights of others from different backgrounds.

Prejudice

In Numbers 12:1 we read: 'Miriam and Aaron began to talk against Moses because of his Cushite wife, for he had married a Cushite.' A Cushite was a black African. I have read some comments on this where prejudice against black Africans is recognised. However, this is probably us bringing our experience of prejudice to the Scripture; while Westerners may have once considered Africans a slave race, in the Nile River valley of ancient Egypt, the Hebrews were the slave race. It is more likely that Miriam and Aaron thought Moses was being presumptuous by marrying above himself.

The prejudice may not therefore have been based on ethnicity but rather on social class!

Theological versus cultural differences.

Paul describes divisions in the church in Corinth in 1 Corinthians 1:10-12. As today we can often fall out along doctrinal lines or because we are drawn to one pastor over another, we can assume this is what was happening in Corinth. It is more likely, though, that the divisions among the members of the church in Corinth were not theological. Let me explain: we may be failing to note ethnic markers that Paul sprinkled all over the text. Apollos was noted as an Alexandrian (Egyptian) Jew (Acts 18:24). They had their own reputation. Paul notes that Peter is called by his Aramaic name, Cephas, suggesting the group that followed him spoke Aramaic and were thus Palestinian Jews. The church would have had Diaspora Jews but also many ethnic Corinthians, who were quite proud of their status as residents of a Roman colony and who enjoyed using Latin. This may explain why Paul doesn't address any theological differences. There weren't any. The problem was ethnic division: Aramaic-speaking Jews, Greek-speaking Jews, Romans and Alexandrians, each with their own faction and faction leader.

This understanding also helps us better understand 1 Corinthians 12 which addresses spiritual gifts, but not just spiritual gifts – verses 12-27 are about unity and diversity in the body. The section begins with a typical Pauline quote about unity amid ethnic and cultural diversity:

> Just as a body, though one, has many parts, but all its many parts form one body, so it is with Christ. For we were all baptised by one Spirit so as to form one body – whether Jews or Gentiles, slave or free – and we were all given the one Spirit to drink. Even so the body is not made up of one part but of many.

The verses that continue speak about how we need all the different parts of the body to function. It is usually understood to be saying that we need different spiritual gifts to function well. However, in the light of how Paul starts this section in verses 12-14, we must be open to the fact that Paul was referring to us needing all the different ethnic groups. The section with verses 21-26 makes much more sense if we see it in the context of how some ethnicities are treated with less respect than others:

> The eye cannot say to the hand, 'I don't need you!' And the head cannot say to the feet, 'I don't need you!' On

the contrary, those parts of the body that seem to be weaker are indispensable, and the parts that we think are less honourable we treat with special honour. And the parts that are unpresentable are treated with special modesty, while our presentable parts need no special treatment. But God has put the body together, giving greater honour to the parts that lacked it, so that there should be no division in the body, but that its parts should have equal concern for each other. If one part suffers, every part suffers with it; if one part is honoured, every part rejoices with it.

(1 Corinthians 12:21-26)

This again seems further evidence to suggest that the divisions described in 1:10-12 are ethnic.

Individual versus corporate interpretations

One major disadvantage in reading the Bible in English is that the English word 'you' can be either singular or plural. Due to our inclination towards individualism, we tend to mostly assume that when we come across 'you' it is singular, which often causes us to misread Scripture and overemphasise our individual relationship with God over and above our corporate relationship with God.

For example, if you understand 1 Corinthians 6:19 (NIV 1984) to mean: 'your [singular] body is a temple of the Holy Spirit, who is in you [singular], whom you [singular] have received from God', you might conclude a good application would be: 'I need to quit smoking.' That is what I had always been told was one appropriate application of this Scripture. If, however, you read: 'your [plural] body is a temple of the Holy Spirit, who is in you [plural], whom you [plural] have received from God', you might conclude Paul's concern has more to do with the community at large. In the context of 1 Corinthians 6, Paul is speaking about visiting temple prostitutes. If you read the passage individually, you think in terms of personal repercussions, but Paul was worried about how bad behaviour contaminated the entire congregation.

Dignity

Matthew, in Matthew 5:39, quotes Jesus as saying that 'if anyone slaps you on the right cheek, turn to them the other cheek also'. I had always understood this to mean that we should not retaliate when attacked, even to be willing to be a punchbag. It never made too much sense to me and wasn't something that I encouraged my children to do. However, I came across a much more convincing interpretation originally from Walter Wink[80] which focused on the explicit mention of the right cheek. He suggested that to slap someone on the right cheek you either had to use your left hand or the back of your right hand. Either way, the implication is that the slap involves an insult; the person being slapped is seen as an inferior. In which case Jesus is saying that if someone treats you as an inferior, insist that you are treated like an equal, that you are treated with dignity.

---

80. Reference is made to this by Wale Hudson-Roberts, 'Just Preaching' in *Intercultural Preaching* (ed. Anthony G. Reddie and Seidel Abel Boanerges with Pamela Searle; Oxford: Centre for Baptist Studies in Oxford), p. 159.

I realise that I am not someone who would normally be the recipient of this kind of slap, I am more likely to be the one doing the slapping, the one failing to treat others with dignity. Therefore, this understanding doesn't come naturally to me in the way it does to those who are from other cultures. I had missed the implication that I should treat everyone with dignity and that others needed to insist that they be treated with dignity. Very different from my previous understanding of what Jesus was teaching.

Money

Our view of money and wealth in the West is very different from other cultures and the context in which the Bible was written.

Outside of the Western world, wealth is often viewed as a limited resource. There is only so much money to be had, so if one person has a lot of it, then everyone else has less to divide among themselves. If you make your slice of pie larger, then my slice is now smaller. In cultures that think in this way, folk are more likely to consider the accumulation of wealth to be immoral, since you can only become wealthy if other people become poor. This is contrasted to the Western view that there is unlimited wealth and so everyone can accumulate as much as they want without impacting anyone else. I can hear you say at this point that we are right in the West! Can I ask you to exercise some humility and listen to the perspective of others, considering others better than ourselves? At the very least it is worth recognising there are other ways of understanding money.

Wealth as a limited resource underpins the way biblical authors viewed the world, for example in Psalm 52:7 where it describes the wicked man who 'trusted in his great wealth and grew strong by destroying others'. In our Western mind, this man demonstrated his wickedness in two ways: he trusted in wealth, and he destroyed others. Yet the psalmist considers these to be one action. This is a type of Hebrew poetry scholars call 'synonymous parallelism', in which the two clauses communicate the same idea with different wording. In other words, hoarding and trusting in wealth was destroying others.

This is a powerful challenge to our perspective on individuals and nations accumulating wealth. We need to be aware that brothers and sisters from other parts of the world will consider the wealth of the West to be a moral issue!

What we wear

Another challenge to my own viewpoint and that of many Western churches is what the Bible means when it encourages us to 'dress modestly' (1 Timothy 2:9).

Westerners routinely misread instructions about modesty in the Bible by assuming sexual modesty is of greater concern than economic modesty. Where sex and money collide, we see which is more important to us – sex. We therefore understand Paul's exhortation that women should dress modestly to mean that their clothes should not be sexually revealing. If we recognise that his concern might instead be economic, then the exhortation is timely for most Western churches, in which everyone keeps their shirts on but in which some dress in ways that say, 'We have more money than you.' This is a way to understand 1 Corinthians 11 where what we wear in worship and how we celebrate the Lord's Supper are addressed. In both cases, the issue is that rich people were flaunting their wealth in the context of worship.

Reaction to changing cultural practices

The costly challenge to cultural ways of thinking is brought out when Peter is told to eat 'unclean' animals in Acts 10.

Peter's reaction to the vision is probably not simply righteous indignation; maybe it is also nausea. No doubt Peter would have been disgusted by the very idea of eating the animals presented in the sheet. Restrictions against eating pork and shellfish are legalities to us. But for first-century Jews, they were deeply entrenched dietary (cultural) ways of life. Peter would have felt as we would if we were confronted with a sheet full of puppies, kittens, bats and cockroaches and told by God, 'Kill and eat.' Like Peter, we would almost certainly reply, 'Surely not, Lord!' (v. 14).

It is reasonable to assume that the faithful Jews who were Jesus' first followers felt much the same way as Peter. Deciding whether Gentile converts to Christianity should follow Jewish dietary laws wasn't simply a theological debate. How were Jewish Christians to share a table of fellowship with people whose breath stank of pig fat?

This again is challenging to us, to allow the Bible to speak to us and for us to be willing to break some strongly held cultural practices that are barriers to the gospel.

My point in this chapter is that we must exercise humility in how we read the Bible, allowing the insights of those from different backgrounds to broaden our understanding and to challenge our preconceived ideas. We need to value the perspective of others and through them, have a more rounded view, maybe even a view that was closer to God's intention for us. This is preferable than for us to see everything through our own cultural lens and end up with our preconceived ideas confirmed. One way to do this is to read widely, especially books written by Christians from other cultures. This is not always easy, as minority authors struggle to get books published. Authors I would commend would include Anthony Reddie, Lamin Sanneh, Soong-Chan Rah, Randolph Richards, Kenneth E. Bailey and Vishal Mangalwadi. Another method I have used is to gather a small group of people from different ethnic backgrounds and to look together at a passage of Scripture and to bring our cultural insights.

Questions to ponder

- How can we ensure we allow the Bible to challenge our culture, rather than reading the Bible through our cultural perspective?
- How can you receive the benefit of the insights of Christians with different cultural perspectives?
- Which preconceived ideas of yours have been challenged in this chapter?

11.

Drawing Things to a Close

It feels the right time to draw things to a conclusion and to commend you for making it this far, unless, of course, you skipped the bit in the middle and went straight to the end.

In this final chapter I want to remind you of the journey we have been on and give some thoughts on where to go next if you want to move forward with building multicultural church.

Amid the general decline in church attendance in the UK, there has been significant growth among ethnic minorities, causing many congregations to go through rapid change. Growth is welcome, but this growth is not without its difficulties and challenges. I have sought to identify some of the great benefits this growth can bring, but also honestly identify the challenges to making the most of this God-given opportunity and give some thoughts on how we can overcome the barriers. In doing so I have sought to paint a picture of the type of churches I believe God would want us to be building in the UK in this season. As a Bible-believing Christian, I have sought to make my case through the lens of Scripture.

The biblical mandate is for us to build united churches that give space for and celebrate diversity; churches that acknowledge we are all made in the image of God and whose distinctives of tribe, culture and language will remain with us through eternity. Gathering and celebrating the many different nations and cultures is great; however, that is only the first step. We need to move beyond uniformity and assimilation.

I have suggested that the default position is that we encourage everyone to assimilate to the majority culture, often but not exclusively white middle class. This happens unless we are purposeful in building something different. Minority groups are absorbed into the larger community, whereby the characteristics that make the newcomers different are lost. Unity is valued, but it can quickly become uniformity and diversity is not valued. Another option values diversity at the expense of unity, with different cultural and ethnic groups worshipping and fellowshipping separately. I believe neither of these options reflect the biblical model of a fully integrated body of Christ that is built on the unity and distinctives found in the Godhead where Father, Son and Spirit are three in one, distinct but in unity. What a model for us to emulate!

Valuing both our distinctives and our oneness in Christ is not easy. It also goes beyond our ethnicity; I have focused on ethnicity, but the principles expounded apply to any fundamental differences. As Paul says, our oneness in Christ includes ethnicity, social class and gender (Galatians 3:28).

I have suggested it is not easy, but it is possible.

New Testament believers appear to have found a way of combining homogeneous people groups with the potential to bridge social divides. This both/and approach held together sameness and diversity, small meetings and larger ones, and intimacy plus exposure to different ideas. Achieving this was far from easy, as the divisions at Corinth demonstrated, but Paul saw it as a priority.[81]

Looking at the experience of the model integrated church in Antioch, I identified some of the barriers that need to be overcome. There is a fear of difference, a fear of what others think of us. 'The fear of difference means that either diversity takes precedence and degenerates into division, or unity gets the upper hand and becomes uniformity.'[82]

Additionally, there are deep-rooted feelings of superiority and inferiority which have developed over generations. In the early church, that was the superiority of Jews over Gentiles. In our context, it can be the superiority of white, middle-class men. In other contexts, it can be one tribe or nation over another. This can be so ingrained that when the pressure comes on, people revert to the default. There needs to be an acknowledgement of this and a desire to move beyond it. Those with privilege need to be willing to use that privilege to lift those without it. Those without privilege need to trust the privileged. Using the prophetic picture presented in Isaiah 11:6 for the wolf to 'live with the lamb', the wolf must forgo his advantages and the lamb has to trust the wolf. This is not trivial. These things need to be explored and understood.

---

81. Michael Moynagh, *Church for Every Context: An Introduction to Theology and Practice* (London: SCM, 2012), Kindle location 918.
82. Moynagh, *Church for Every Context*, Kindle location 4845.

We do this not just to build churches that reflect God and bring the future into the present, we also do it because we are called to be the 'light of the world' (Matthew 5:14), shining God's light into the darkness. The world around us is in darkness, struggling to come to terms with ethnic conflict; we have light to bring into that darkness. We cannot afford to abdicate our responsibility to model how to build deep, healthy relationships with those who are different from us.

We need to recognise our prejudices, understanding that racism and other forms of prejudice are not binary; it is not as simple as you are either prejudiced or not. It is a continuum; we are all prejudiced to a certain extent. Prejudice is therefore something that needs to be identified, acknowledged and continually overcome, it is not a once-and-for-all activity. There needs to be ongoing work of repentance and forgiveness if we are to move towards the types of churches that God requires.

We also need to acknowledge that as we seek to overcome the barriers to unity while valuing diversity, we have an enemy, Satan, who seeks to thwart God's purposes. If God wants a church that demonstrates our oneness in Christ, Satan will do all he can to sow divisions. As Paul says, 'Our struggle is not against flesh and blood, but against the rulers, against the authorities, against the powers of this dark world and against the spiritual forces of evil in the heavenly realms' (Ephesians 6:12). Not only does our enemy attack us as individuals, he is also at work in society and even in churches through principalities and powers. We shouldn't therefore be surprised that things such as institutional racism can exist within society and in the church. We shouldn't just dismiss such things as 'wokism', but recognise the work of the enemy and seek to stand up to it using all the weapons we have been given. It is a spiritual battle we are engaged in.

It is a battle worth fighting, not just to demonstrate the kingdom but also for effective evangelism. John records Jesus as praying, 'My prayer is not for them alone. I pray also for those who will believe in me through their message, that all of them may be one, Father, just as you are in me and I am in you. May they also be in us so that the world may believe that you have sent me' (John 17:20-21). Our unity in diversity is a factor in the world believing that Jesus has been sent by God. The world sees something of the glorious bride of Christ in all its radiant, multicultural splendour and sees something of the glory of God. We have to ask, to what extent has our divided church inhibited our evangelism? If we want to see our nation re-evangelised, then churches that value everyone made in the image of God, churches that value our distinctives, are going to play a major role.

I believe the most important characteristic that is needed for us to build integrated churches is humility. To become a Christian, we need humility in accepting our inability to save ourselves, and our need of a Saviour. Jesus was characterised by his humility. It should also be at the heart of who we are, considering others as better than ourselves (see Philippians 2:3). Without humility we cannot move forward, but with it everything is possible. Yet dealing with our pride is not easy. Integrated, multicultural churches require humility; they also help us grow in humility!

Humility enables and requires us to learn from people who are different from us. If an elephant and a mouse are locked together in a room, the mouse is motivated to know everything it can about the elephant, for fear of being trampled. The elephant has no need to learn about the mouse. Minorities are motivated to learn about the majority; it requires humility for the majority to spend time learning about other cultures – there is no felt need to do so. It is essential they do if we are to build fully integrated churches.

We need to expand our understanding of culture generally; how many people newly arrived in our country will be suffering symptoms of culture shock, and how can we help them? We need to understand the general characteristics of different cultures and how they impact expectations of church life. As leaders, we need to understand these things and then help others understand them.

I believe passionately that we also need to listen to people who are different from us, to put ourselves in their shoes. Listening to different ethnic minorities, we see that history is more important to them than for many of the majority culture. We can easily dismiss slavery and colonisation as ancient history, but that is not the case for those who feel their lives are still impacted by them. As the beneficiaries of privilege, we can be blind to the biblical theme of justice, which is so relevant and important to those who are the victims of injustice. It is sobering to recognise that some of the injustices have been perpetrated in the name of Jesus.

Finally, I looked at ways our understanding of what the Bible teaches can be enriched and challenged through the perspective of others. Through a handful of examples, we explored the benefits of humbly learning from the perspectives of others as we study the Scriptures. Through that we discover more of the richness that exists in the diverse people of God.

To close...

I want to look at a practical starting point to help us move towards reconciliation.

John Perkins in his book *One Blood* identifies five elements that are essential for the reconciliation that is needed for us to be able to fully trust and learn from each other: lament, confession, forgiveness, prayer and love.

Lament

Lament is acknowledging that things are not how they are meant to be. We lament the damage caused by racism, the divisions in the church, our failure to give a lead to the world but rather have been wrongly influenced by the world. We recognise all these are wrong. The way things are in so many ways is not how God wanted things to be. It is appropriate that we should feel pain because of it, because God himself is pained. As Paul says:

> We know that the whole creation has been groaning as in the pains of childbirth right up to the present time. Not only so, but we ourselves, who have the firstfruits of the Spirit, groan inwardly as we wait eagerly for our adoption to sonship, the redemption of our bodies. For in this hope we were saved. But hope that is seen is no hope at all. Who hopes for what they already have?
>
> *(Romans 8:22-24)*

We groan inwardly about what is happening, about what has happened; we, with all of God's creation, groan. We have something better to hope for, but for now we can and should groan. We should lament.

More than one-third of the psalms are laments. They allow the psalmist to cry out to God in anguish, knowing that God alone is the ultimate healer and justifier.

The psalms teach us to lament; they allow and encourage us to vent our sadness, our anger and our frustration. They enable us to express our feelings to release our tears; tears that are part of our healing. The psalms of lament usually start with a desperate cry; there is then a petition, a request for help before concluding with praise.

So, an initial Christian response to the challenges, the pain all around us, starts with lament.

We need to feel pain because God feels pain; pain for the fact that things are not as they are meant to be. We need to take that pain to God.

Confession

We need to start with lament but to move on from lament. We need to also recognise our role, our contribution to the problems of the world. We are each both victims and perpetrators. We acknowledge the fact that we are perpetrators before dwelling on our victimhood. This is the second element of our journey.

'Brokenness is the opposite of pride. It is the willingness to admit our faults without concern for our reputation. It is the willingness to lay down our own rights and do whatever benefits the other. It is putting the needs of the other above our own. It lays the groundwork for reconciliation to occur.'[83]

For me, a white, well-educated man, I need to confess that I have used my advantages to benefit myself. I have in so many ways added to the weight others have to carry. For so many years, when I was unaware of those advantages, I was filled with pride like the Pharisee in the parable from Luke 18:9-14.

I must confess my racist thoughts and actions, to ask forgiveness from God and from others. I must confess my lack of actions, taking my advantages for granted as if somehow I deserved them.

Let us each examine ourselves. What have we contributed to the issues we see around us? Maybe you have allowed anger and resentment to rise within you because of how you have been treated. Maybe you have looked down on certain groups of people also made in the image of God.

John Perkins shares about his need to confess his anger resulting from the way he was treated, and especially how white policemen murdered his brother.[84] My examples, maybe your examples, feel trivial in comparison, but they are no less real and important.

Have you felt anger waiting for hours and hours in a queue at the accident and emergency (A&E) department, waiting to be seen? Treating staff badly, because of frustration. Seeking to blame someone.

Have you applied for job after job and seemingly been passed over, either because you are an ethnic minority and you feel you have been discriminated against, or because you

---

83. Perkins, *One Blood*, p. 81.
84. Perkins, *One Blood*, p. 81.

are white and feel that ethnic minorities are now being given jobs because of some 'woke' agenda? Are you struggling to make ends meet, or know of others struggling to afford to put their heating on while asylum seekers are being housed in hotels, and feeling anger and resentment because of it? Is there anger and resentment that you need to confess?

In a recent book, *'Tis Mercy All*, Natalie Williams[85] speaks about the breadth of mercy that was offered by Jesus. He offered mercy to so-called bad guys, the oppressing Romans or religious leaders, the unclean lepers and adulterers, the exploitative tax collectors or people like the Samaritans, from the places we despise. He didn't seem to care about offending anyone by mixing with their enemies.

She challenges us to do the same, to offer mercy to even bad guys, recognising that for some, offering mercy to the poor and needy will come more easily but offering mercy to oppressors may be more difficult. For others, it will be the other way around. Personally, I find it hard to offer mercy to certain people – for example, the extreme right wing and those I perceive as racist. Yet I must admit that Jesus had a different attitude to mine and that I need to change to be more like him, having received his undeserved mercy myself. I recognised my need to confess my lack of mercy and compassion.

There is so much we all need to confess.

Perkins again:

---

85. Natalie Williams, *'Tis Mercy All: The Power of Mercy in a Polarised World* (London: SPCK, 2024), Kindle edition, p. 46.

They say that confession is good for the soul. I believe this to be true. I believe that it is good for us as individuals – and that it is good for the soul of the church. But it's not just good – it's essential. It is essential if we are to be reconciled one with another. It opens the door for the healing balm of forgiveness to wash over us. Let's go there next. Let's go there together.[86]

We all need to lament; we all need to confess. We are all perpetrators; we are all victims. Confession, then, leads us and allows us to forgive.

Forgiveness

There is something important and profound to start by recognising and acknowledging our role as a perpetrator before recognising we are also a victim. It brings things into a different perspective – a truly Christian perspective.

As victims, the essential Christian response is forgiveness. That is the third step of the journey. As Perkins said, it is good to take the step of forgiveness together. Forgiveness is the heart of all we believe. Christ has forgiven us – he paid the price for us as perpetrators. He forgives our sins: 'as far as the east is from the west, so far has he removed our transgressions from us' (Psalm 103:12).

We are, then, called to forgive those who have sinned against us. While we have no control over what others have done to us, we have complete control and responsibility for how we respond.

---

86. Perkins, *One Blood*, p. 93.

Corrie ten Boom shared this concerning her work with those who were victims of the Holocaust: 'Those who were able to forgive their former enemies were able also to return to the outside world and rebuild their lives, no matter what the physical scars. Those who nursed their bitterness remained invalids. It was as simple and as horrible as that.'[87]

I know this is hard. Whenever we are victims of racism or some other form of prejudice, events continually bring feelings of hurt back. Every time we are discriminated against, it reminds us of past events.

Israel Olofinjana describes his ongoing feelings of discrimination:

> How, then, is Britishness perceived by the general public? There is a normative idea among the public that to be British, or particularly to be English, is to be white. This is demonstrated through many white British attitudes that do not accept any non-white people as British. Therefore, if your ethnicity is Asian British or black British, you are rejected as not being British. An example of this attitude was revealed during the Channel Four documentary *Make Bradford British* in which an Asian British lady was criticised by white British people in a pub. The criticism, which reduced her to tears, centred on questioning her identity as a British Pakistani Muslim. The white British simply told her that she was not British because she was a Muslim from a Pakistani background.[88]

---

87. https://guideposts.org/positive-living/guideposts-classics-corrie-ten-boom-forgiveness/ (accessed 28.10.24).
88. Olofinjana, ed., *Turning the Tables on Mission*, Kindle location 1781.

I know that such experiences keep bringing up all those feelings of hurt and anger and frustration, not just when they happen to us, but also when they are recounted by others. The process of forgiveness is usually not a once-and-for-all episode, it is something that must be repeated regularly. The alternative is bitterness and anger.

The forgiveness required may be because you have been falsely accused of racism, or feel your way of life has been lost because of immigration. Having confessed your anger, we need to move on to forgive, together.

Let us never trivialise the process and cost of forgiveness. It cost Christ his life; he died that we could be forgiven. As we have been forgiven so much, we should forgive others. We need to forgive others.

Prayer

Having lamented, acknowledged things are not as God intended, confessed our role in that and forgiven those we are able to forgive, we have a foundation from which we can move forward to the fourth step of the journey – prayer, intercession. Our prayer will be different than if we hadn't gone on this journey.

We can bring what appears to be insurmountable issues to our powerful and immense God, who is the ultimate healer and justifier. He will 'wipe every tear' from our eyes (Revelation 21:4). He will bring justice. He is the hope of the world.

We are not powerless. We have the King of kings, the Maker of heaven and earth on our side. Let's bring the challenges of the world back to him.

Increasingly I am convinced that prayer is the answer. 'Is prayer your steering wheel or your spare tyre?'[89] Too often prayer is a last resort, something we do in an emergency, or extreme circumstances. The state of the world, the needs of the world, ensure that prayer is at the heart of our lives: 'God shapes the world by prayer. The more praying there is in the world the better the world will be, the mightier the forces against evil.'[90] In a quote attributed to Billy Graham, the evangelist said, 'To get nations back on their feet, we must first get down on our knees.'[91]

We need to be praying as individuals and as a church for the world that we are in. The psalms often start with lament; they then move on to prayer, petition, asking for God to intervene. We need to be praying in this way too, for ourselves, for our churches, for our nation.

Intercession shouldn't lead to passivity, but to action. God uses us to answer our prayers.

The final step of the journey is therefore love.

Love

Perkins, reflecting on the example of Jesus, says:

> And the idea of Him forgiving the very ones who were killing Him and praying for them while they were doing it . . . well, if you think about that long enough, it will change you. It will force you to get outside yourself and ask if you are willing to love others the same way.[92]

---

89. Attributed to Corrie ten Boom. Original quote not found.
90. Attributed to E.M. Bounds and also Mother Teresa. Original quote not found.
91. Widely quoted but original quote not found.
92. Perkins, *One Blood*, p. 161.

I came across a powerful African proverb: 'When I saw you from afar, I thought you were a monster. When you got closer, I thought you were just an animal. When you got even closer, I saw that you were a human. But when we were face to face, I realised that you were my brother.'

We offer something different from the world, a world of conflict and hatred, a world of prejudice and pain. We offer love, the love of Christ. We need to love people as brothers. As Jesus said, 'A new command I give you: love one another. As I have loved you, so you must love one another. By this everyone will know that you are my disciples, if you love one another' (John 13:34-35). He went further, as recorded in Matthew's Gospel – we need to love everyone, even our enemies:

> You have heard that it was said, 'Love your neighbour and hate your enemy.' But I tell you, love your enemies and pray for those who persecute you, that you may be children of your Father in heaven. He causes his sun to rise on the evil and the good, and sends rain on the righteous and the unrighteous ...
>
> *(Matthew 5:43-48)*

It doesn't happen easily. Hence the journey. Yet the journey does equip us to make a difference in this broken world. To be Christ, the body of Christ, in this dark place. The journey helps us avoid despair, helps us avoid indifference and leads us to be instruments for good, empowered by the Holy Spirit. The journey allows us to build churches that are united in love for one another while celebrating our differences. The journey enables us to overcome the barriers that we put up between ourselves and those who are different from us. It allows us to overcome Satan and the discord he sows.

And we don't just need to go on the journey as individuals but together as the people of God. That is our calling together.

This is a distinctive Christian response.

To lament, to confess, to forgive, to pray and then to love.

> ## Questions to ponder
>
> - How can you incorporate the journey of lament, confession, forgiveness, prayer, love into your lifestyle and that of your church?
> - What would be three simple things that you could implement to give greater value to ethnic diversity?
> - What are the key takeaways for you from the book?

www.ingramcontent.com/pod-product-compliance
Lightning Source LLC
Chambersburg PA
CBHW070147100426
42743CB00013B/2838